A Prayer for Owen Meany

A novel by John Irving
adapted by Simon Bent

NT
TRANS
FORM
AT!ON

A Prayer for
Owen Meany

A novel by John Irving
adapted by Simon Bent

In order of speaking

John Wheelwright	RICHARD HOPE
Barb Wiggins	HARRIET THORPE
Girl	REBECCA VERE
Boy	DANIEL TUITE
Mary Beth	DEBBIE CHAZEN
Harold Crosby	RAFE SPALL
Owen Meany	AIDAN McARDLE
Grandma (Harriet Wheelwright)	GILLIAN BARGE
Tabitha Wheelwright	KELLY REILLY
Mr Meany	ROBIN SOANS
Mrs Meany	SANDY McDADE
Rector Wiggins	STUART MILLIGAN
Reverend Merrill	HUGH ROSS
Lydia	MARLENE SIDAWAY
Dan Needham	DEMETRI GORITSAS
Mr Fish	MICHAEL BRAY
Coach Chickering	RAFE SPALL
Chief Pike	DANIEL TUITE
Randy White	MICHAEL BRAY
Sam White, his wife	REBECCA VERE
Larry Lish	RAFE SPALL
Mitzy Lish, his mother	HARRIET THORPE
Dr Dolder	ROBIN SOANS
Jarvit Mother	HARRIET THORPE
Jarvit Daughter	REBECCA VERE
Jarvit Father	MICHAEL BRAY
Jarvit Son	DANIEL TUITE
Major Rawls	STUART MILLIGAN

Other parts played by members of the Company

Director	MICK GORDON
Designer	DICK BIRD
Lighting Designer	NEIL AUSTIN
Soundtrack	JON FRANKEL
Sound Designer	NEIL ALEXANDER
Company Voice Work	PATSY RODENBURG & KATE GODFREY

Assistant Director (Cohen Bursary)	Tim Stark
Production Manager	Digby Robinson
Stage Manager	Alison Rankin
Deputy Stage Manager	David Milling
Assistant Stage Managers	Emma Gordon, Richard Reddrop
Assistant to the Lighting Designer	Cathy Joyce
Costume Supervisor	Caroline Waterman assisted by Sara Wan
Casting	Gabrielle Dawes

OPENING: Lyttelton 13 June 2002

LENGTH: about 2 hours 45 minutes, including two 15-minute intervals

THE ACTION TAKES PLACE MAINLY IN THE TOWN OF GRAVESEND, NEW HAMPSHIRE, NEW ENGLAND, BETWEEN 1953 AND 1968

NATIONAL THEATRE STUDIO &
TRANSFORMATION

Royal National Theatre
South Bank, London SE1 9PX
Box Office: 020 7452 3000
Information: 020 7452 3400

Registered Charity No: 224223

Many of the projects in the Transformation season were developed in the National Theatre Studio, and all the plays in the Loft are National Theatre Studio co-productions.

The Studio is the National's laboratory for research and development, providing a workspace outside the confines of the rehearsal room and stage, where artists can experiment and develop their skills.

As part of its training for artists there is an on-going programme of classes, workshops, seminars, courses and masterclasses. Residencies have also been held in Edinburgh, Vilnius, Belfast and South Africa thus enabling artists from a wider community to share and exchange experiences.

Central to the Studio's work is a commitment to new writing. The development and support of writers is demonstrated through play readings, workshops, short-term attachments, bursaries and sessions with senior writers. Work developed there continually reaches audiences throughout the country and overseas, on radio, film and television as well as at the National and other theatres.

For the Royal National Theatre Studio

HEAD OF STUDIO
Sue Higginson

STUDIO MANAGER
Matt Strevens

TECHNICAL MANAGER
Eddie Keogh

INTERNATIONAL PROJECTS MANAGER
Philippe Le Moine

The chief aims of the National, under the direction of Trevor Nunn, are to present a diverse repertoire, embracing classic, new and neglected plays; to present these plays to the very highest standards; and to give audiences a wide choice.

All kinds of other events and services are on offer – short early-evening Platform performances; work for children and education work; free live entertainment both inside and outdoors at holiday times; exhibitions; live foyer music; backstage tours; bookshops; plenty of places to eat and drink; and easy car-parking. The nearby Studio acts as a resource for research and development for actors, writers and directors.

We send productions on tour, both in this country and abroad, and do all we can, through ticket-pricing, to make the NT accessible to everyone.

The National's home on the South Bank, opened in 1976, contains three separate theatres: the Olivier, the Lyttelton, and the Cottesloe and – during Transformation – a fourth: the Loft. It is open to the public all day, six days a week, fifty-two weeks a year. Stage by Stage – an exhibition on the NT's history, can be seen in the Olivier Gallery.

First published in this adaptation in 2002 by Oberon Books Ltd.
(incorporating Absolute Classics)
521 Caledonian Road, London N7 9RH
Tel: 020 7607 3637 / Fax: 020 7607 3629

e-mail: oberon.books@btinternet.com

A catalogue record for this book is available from the British
Library.

ISBN: 1 84002 334 1

Proofread by Prufrock – www.prufrock.co.uk

Printed in Great Britain by Antony Rowe Ltd., Chippenham.

Characters

JOHN WHEELWRIGHT

OWEN MEANY

BARB WIGGINS

GIRL ONE

BOY ONE

HAROLD CROSBY

MARY BETH

GRANDMOTHER

TABITHA WHEELWRIGHT

MR MEANY

MRS MEANY

RECTOR WIGGINS

REVEREND MERRILL

LYDIA

DAN NEEDHAM

MR FISH

COACH CHICKERING

CHIEF PIKE

RANDY WHITE

SAM WHITE

LARRY LISH

MRS LISH

DOCTOR DOLDER

MAJOR RAWLS

JARVIT FATHER

JARVIT MOTHER

JARVIT DAUGHTER

JARVIT BOY

NUNS

CHILDREN

The main action of the play takes place in the town of
Gravesend, New Hampshire, New England between 1953
and 1968

Note
The text is correct at time of going to press, but may differ
slightly from the play as performed

ACT ONE

Enter JOHN. Walks downstage. Enter OWEN. Pushing on a large chair upstage.

John I am doomed to remember a boy with a wrecked voice – not because of his voice or because he was the smallest person I ever knew or even because he was the instrument of my mother's death, but because he is the reason I believe in God. I am a Christian because of Owen Meany.

OWEN climbs up on chair and sits with legs sticking out. Enter BARB WIGGINS with Bible.

Barb The Lord Jesus Christ died on the cross for our sins, children, and it is to him that we must give over our lives. Remember what the Bible says, children.

She opens bible.

John I don't read the Bible anymore.

Barb (*Reads.*) Whosoever liveth and believeth in me shall never die.

John I read the Book of Common Prayer.

Barb (*Reads.*) We bring nothing into this world, and it is certain that we carry nothing out. The pain, the suffering, the body of Christ, the blood, the wounds, the stigmata – I want you to think about this, children.

A row of children on wooden Sunday school chairs, their feet touching the floor. An empty chair at the end of the row. BARB WIGGINS stands before them with an open Bible.

Children Yes mam.

Barb Silently and seriously, that's how I want you to think.

Children Yes mam.

Shuts bible.

Barb I'm going to leave you alone with your thoughts now, children.

Children Yes mam.

Barb Our Lord on the Cross, children.

Children Yes mam.

Barb I want you to think very hard about this. And when I get back we'll talk about it.

John Yes mam.

JOHN sits. Exit BARB.

Girl One Owen Meany, you're so cute.

Boy One He's a Catholic.

Girl One Those legs.

Mary Beth Like a doll.

Harold Catholic.

Boy One Catholic's ain't got no livers, that's why they're mean, Meany.

Harold Yeah, I got chased by a Catholic with a frying pan once, he sure as hell didn't have no liver – boy was he mean.

Mary Beth He's so light, let's pick him up.

Boy One Pick him up, Mary Beth.

Harold Pick up the doll.

They pick up OWEN and pass him over their heads.

John Leave him alone.

Boy One What's it to you, Johnny Wheelwright.

John He's my friend.

Boy One You're a Congressionalist.

Girl One No he is not, Johnny Wheelwright is a
Congregationalist – they're like Methodists, only more so.

Mary Beth Like a doll.

Girl One So cute.

Mary Beth He's so light.

OWEN rises above them and hangs suspended in mid-air.

Boy One Johnny Wheelwright – he hasn't got a father.

Harold Neither have you.

Boy One Yeah but my daddy's dead, he died killing the
Japs – he never had one.

Harold Oh.

Boy One You're a Congressionalist, we're Episcopalians.

Harold Yeah.

Mary Beth Like a rag doll.

Harold Jap doll.

Owen (*Piercing, shrill, blood-curdling.*) Put me down. Cut it out. I don't want to do this anymore. Enough is enough. Put me down, you assholes.

Enter GRANDMOTHER. Small knife in one hand, potato in the other.

Grandmother Whatever you're doing up there, whatever it is you're doing to that poor boy to make him sound like that, stop it you hear me, stop it at once.

Exit CHILDREN except for JOHN. OWEN left in mid-air as if hanging from a coat peg in a large dark cupboard.

Owen (*Shrill.*) Get me down from here.

TABITHA at one end of a long kitchen table in flaming red dress. At the other end potatoes and peelings on newspaper next to a pan of water in front of GRANDMOTHER.

Grandmother Do it now, John.

John But Grandma.

Tabitha He's only playing mother.

Grandmother He's your son, but it's my house.

GRANDMOTHER cotinues peeling potatoes.

John Do my math homework and I'll let you down.

Owen That's blackmail.

John Yes.

Owen No.

Tabitha It looked so pretty in the shop window but now, I don't know – I just don't know.

Grandmother Try peeling a potato.

Owen Turn on the light, something's licking my face, turn on the light, something with a tongue, something is licking me.

John It's just a cobweb.

Owen It's too wet for a cobweb, it's a tongue, turn on the light.

John Do my math homework.

OWEN lets out a cry from hell.

Tabitha John.

John Mom.

Tabitha Are you hanging Owen from the peg in your grandpa's closet again.

John Yes, mom.

Tabitha Well fetch him down, now.

John Yes, mom.

OWEN lowered to the ground. As he is lowered, cards drop from his pockets.

Owen My baseball cards.

Grandmother The wail of a banshee and the legs of Pinocchio. (*Nicks herself peeling a potato.*) Oooh.

Owen Pick them up.

Grandmother Damn and blast this potato.

Owen Pick up my cards.

Tabitha You don't have to do that.

Grandmother I like doing it.

Tabitha That's what we've got a cook for.

Grandmother She doesn't do them right.

OWEN now on the ground.

Owen Pick up my baseball cards.

John You don't like baseball.

Owen Whether I like baseball or not is irrelevant, the point is it's a man's world out there, you know about baseball you can walk into a bar anywhere anyplace and talk to anyone, you'll get along just fine – you can't talk baseball and you're all washed up. As it happens, I also like the smell of them.

OWEN and JOHN pick up cards. GRANDMOTHER holds up peeled potato.

Grandmother Irish, like that boy up there, that friend of your son's.

TABITHA does a twirl.

Tabitha What do you think.

Grandmother That boy –

Tabitha Owen.

Grandmother You always stick up for him.

Tabitha I like him. What do you think.

Grandmother That boy comes from a long line of Irish peasants. The Wheelwrights were on the Mayflower, we founded this town, we helped found this country and now a son of yours is playing upstairs with the son of an Irish quarryman.

Tabitha They own the granite quarry, mother.

Grandmother They don't wash.

Tabitha They wash.

Grandmother A son of yours.

Tabitha New Hampshire is 'The Granite State'.

Grandmother And it's principal business is tree.

Tabitha Daddy made it big in shoes.

Grandmother His decision not to unionize the factory is legendary.

Tabitha This dress isn't too long.

Grandmother A son of yours. He must take after his father.

Tabitha Don't. I've told you all I'm ever going to tell you on that subject.

Grandmother That the father of my grandchild is a man you met once on the Boston and Maine train while going to a singing lesson.

Tabitha Yes.

Grandmother And you haven't seen him since.

Tabitha What do you think of my dress.

Grandmother So it could be anyone.

Tabitha I'm not sure about the colour.

Grandmother So when I hand over my ticket for inspection on the Boston and Maine railway and the conductor says, 'Thank you mam,' I could be talking to the father of my grandson.

Tabitha If that's what you think.

Grandmother No it is not what I think, what I think is that you should avoid travelling on the Boston and Maine railway.

Tabitha I have to, for my singing.

Grandmother I blame the Reverend Merrill, singing lessons instead of a college education – I was too distracted, your father was busy dying at the time and he needed my help – he was never an easy man to help do anything… And another thing I think is that every time I see that boy –

Tabitha Owen.

Grandmother I just want to rip off those dusty old clothes –

Tabitha They live next to a quarry.

Grandmother I don't care, it's no excuse – burn those clothes, stick him in the bath and scrub him with carbolic.

Tabitha You like him.

Grandmother I dislike no one.

Tabitha You like him.

Grandmother I don't.

Tabitha You do.

Grandmother No, I do not – put these potatoes on the stove.

Tabitha What do you think. I don't like the colour. I'm not sure of the colour. Does it suit me. What do you think.

Grandmother Very pretty.

Tabitha I'll go and take it off.

TABITHA goes to exit.

Grandmother And don't forget the potatoes.

Tabitha No, I won't.

TABITHA returns and picks up potatoes.

Grandmother It suits you. The colour, the cut and everything.

Tabitha You think so.

Grandmother I just said so.

Tabitha You're not just saying that.

Grandmother No.

TABITHA puts down pan and kisses GRANDMOTHER.

Tabitha I love you.

TABITHA picks up pan and exits.

Grandmother Lord help us, Lord help us all, especially those that help themselves.

Wraps up peelings.

Exit GRANDMOTHER.

Owen For a Congregationalist like you to turn Episcopalian it's nothing, just a move upward in church formality, in hocus pocus – but for a Catholic like me it's a move away from the hocus pocus and you run the risk of eternal damnation. My father will be damned and burn in hell for rejecting the Church of Rome. But they started it, the Catholics committed the unspeakable outrage – they insulted my mom and dad beyond repair.

John Why, what did they do.

Owen Nothing. And I don't like being hung on a peg in your grandpa's closet.

John You said you did.

Owen Well not anymore, okay.

John Okay. We'll go and play at your house from now on.

Owen No, we won't.

John Why not.

Owen And I would have done your math homework anyway, I promised your mom.

John Why can't we play at your house.

Owen We can.

A loud blast of TNT offstage. A fine grey dust falls, descending on the boys.

John You like my mom.

Owen I love your mom.

Another explosion.

MRS MEANY sitting on a chair next to a phonograph listening to it. She is wearing a First World War leather flying hat with the ear-flaps down. Expressionless and grey.

Enter MR MEANY, black suit covered in grey dust.

A fine grey dust falls, descending on MRS MEANY and MR MEANY.

A letter falls from above.

Silence between them.

Music.

Mr Meany It's a letter.

He picks up letter. She turns up phonograph.

Damn phonograph. Where's Owen.

Mrs Meany Out.

Mr Meany He's always out.

Mrs Meany Out playing.

Mr Meany With rich letter-writing folk. We're not good enough for him. We've never been good enough for him.

Mrs Meany We were blessed.

Mr Meany Cursed.

Blast of TNT offstage.

She turns up phonograph.

He turns it off.

Damn phonograph.

Mrs Meany You don't like it, tell them to stop blasting.

Mr Meany The day they stop blasting is the day we stop eating. (*Pause.*) When you die I'm getting a dog.

Mrs Meany Get one now, who's stopping you, I'm not stopping you.

Mr Meany I will.

MR MEANY sits. A loud blast of TNT offstage. Fine cloud of grey dust descends on the MEANYS. He looks at letter.

It's a letter.

OWEN and JOHN enter. OWEN is in underpants. Clothes piled at side. Throwing rocks in quarry pool.

Owen Some of these quarry pools just keep on going down and down and down and down and don't ever stop.

John I'll never get to know who my real dad is.

Owen Yes you will. To the centre of the earth.

John No, I won't. Where did you learn to throw like that.

Owen Nowhere, it just comes natural.

John He doesn't care.

Owen You don't know that, you've never met him.

John Because he doesn't care.

Owen One day, one day when it's right he will be identified to you.

John How do you know.

Owen I know.

John Because you talk to God.

OWEN skims stones.

Owen Go on, then.

JOHN skims a stone, half-hearted.

Your father can hide from you but he can't hide from God.

John You talk to God.

Owen You don't believe me.

Enter BOY ONE and HAROLD CROSBY, GIRL ONE and MARY BETH, in underwear and T-shirts. BOY ONE carries a long, coiled rope. He throws rope on ground.

Boy One We got the rope.

Mary Beth You don't have to, Owen.

Owen I want to.

OWEN picks up rope and ties it round his waist.

Boy One Swim the pool, Meany.

Owen I'm going to, and then I'm going to kiss your sister.

Boy One Nobody kisses my sister.

Mary Beth Kiss me instead, I don't have a brother.

Owen I'll kiss you as well, Mary Beth.

Boy One Dirty filthy little Catholic.

Owen Give me the rope.

MARY BETH picks up other end of rope.

One tug and you haul me in.

Boy One Sure thing, Owen.

Owen If anything happens, anything at all, you swim out and get me.

OWEN walks to water's edge and rope uncoils.

Mr Meany A letter from the Town Committee. First there's their interests and then there's mine. Them and us, it's them and us.

MRS MEANY turns off phonograph.

Damn phonograph.

MR MEANY opens letter and reads it.

OWEN at edge of stage. OWEN exits. As he does the rope goes taut.

Harold He's in the water. He's swimming.

BOY ONE slaps HAROLD across the head.

What. What did I do.

Mary Beth Help me, help me with the rope.

They all take hold of rope. They feed the rope as OWEN swims out.

Mr Meany (*Reads.*) 'Dear Mr Meany, Regarding the Committee's decision to widen the Squamscott river to ease the passage of boating crews from the Gravesend Academy for Boys and your refusal to co-operate.' …underlined, I like that – what do you think, Mrs Meany.

Mrs Meany I don't think anything, I pray for salvation.

Mr Meany There's no salvation without repentence, and I ain't repenting.

Mrs Meany It's for Owen that I pray.

Mr Meany The Devil is my shepherd.

Mrs Meany I pray for Owen.

Mr Meany Not after the unspeakable outrage that He has committed, Him and His Church.

He looks at letter.

'The Committee has decided' …to hell with the Committee, to hell with the Gravesend Academy for Boys – it's my land, they can't touch it without my say, the only thing they're getting from me is a gravestone and it won't be for nothing. It's my land.

Mrs Meany It's mud.

Mr Meany My mud.

Mrs Meany Owen wants to try for the Academy.

Mr Meany That boy's going to learn to cut granite. Your God's Son was a carpenter, if woodworking was good enough for Jesus then granite's good enough for Owen.

MRS MEANY turns up phonograph.

Damn phonograph.

Silence between them. Music.

It's them and us I'm talking about –

Screws up letter.

Them and us.

Exit MR MEANY.

The rope suddenly goes very taut and they struggle to keep hold of it.

Mary Beth He's tugging.

John Pull him in, pull.

They pull. Then just as suddenly, the rope goes very slack. They pull in the rope. No OWEN.

I can't see him.

Silence.

Boy One Nothing.

John Nothing.

Boy One Not even a ripple.

Silence.

John Go and get him.

Harold You go get him.

Mary Beth I'll go and get him.

Harold You can't swim.

Enter OWEN dripping wet.

Owen Talk about hurting someone's feelings – what were you waiting for, bubbles – what do you think I am, a fish – wasn't anyone going to come and get me.

Silence.

Well.

John You scared us, Owen.

Owen You let me drown. You didn't do anything. You just watched me drown. I'm already dead. Remember that – you let me die.

John Where were you.

Owen You let me die. You killed me, I'm dead.

John It was a test.

Owen Yes, it was a test and you killed me.

OWEN picks up his clothes. Exit OWEN. Exit BOY ONE, HAROLD, GIRL ONE and MARY BETH.

Music.

John (*To audience.*) And I felt sad not because I was sad but for the future when I knew I would miss him, he'd be gone – and I was filled with doubt. I didn't believe in angels then, I do now, I have to. I left the Episcopalian…

JOHN gets dressed. Enter RECTOR WIGGINS and REVEREND MERRILL at opposite sides of the stage.

Wiggins I am the resurrection and the life, saith the Lord: he that believeth in me, though he were dead, yet he shall live: and whosoever liveth and believeth in me, shall never die.

John I left the Congregationalists…

Merrill God the F-F-F-Father, God the Son, God the Holy Ghost, bless, preserve, and keep you: the Lord mercifully with his favour look upon you, and fill you with all spiritual b-b-b-benediction and grace; that ye may so live together in this life, that in the world to come ye may have life everlasting. Amen.

Wiggins God spake these words, and said –

Enter GRANDMOTHER.

Grandmother Set the table in the drawing room for aperitifs, it's Thanksgiving and we've got guests coming.

A long table set.

Merrill I am the Lord thy God; Thou shalt have none other gods but me.

Grandmother Lydia!

Wiggins Let us pray.

Grandmother Lydia!

Wiggins/Merrill (*Together.*) I believe in one God, the Father Almighty, Maker of Heaven and earth, And of all things visible and invisible.

Grandmother John, is your friend staying for Thanksgiving.

John Yes, Grandma.

Enter TABITHA.

Wiggins Amen.

Merrill Amen.

Tabitha His name is Owen.

Grandmother What sort of a name's that.

Tabitha It's a good name.

Grandmother It's not in the Bible. Lydia!

Enter LYDIA in a wheelchair.

Lydia I've only got two wheels.

Grandmother You were slower when you had legs.

Lydia I don't know why I stay around here a moment longer than I have to.

Grandmother Because you're family.

Lydia No, I'm not. I'm just a stupid old cook who's lost both her legs through no fault of her own. I should have taken full advantage of my legs while I still had them and got married.

Grandmother But there was no one asking, Lydia.

Lydia There was Mr Fish.

Grandmother Mr Fish is an atheist.

Lydia Yes – and he killed his first wife, and then his dog, and then he would have killed me and I'd have gone straight to hell and then you'd feel bad.

Tabitha Mr Fish did not kill his wife.

Lydia What do you know – aperitifs in the drawing room, whoever heard of such a thing.

Tabitha I'm going to make an announcement.

Lydia What sort of announcement.

Tabitha Wait and see.

Lydia I remember the last announcement.

John When was that.

Lydia Nine months before you were born.

Grandmother Owen's staying for Thanksgiving.

Lydia We won't have enough turkey.

Grandmother Nonsense, the turkey's bigger than Owen.

Lydia He can help with the drinks.

Enter OWEN, BARB WIGGINS, WIGGINS and MERRILL. OWEN carries a tray of drinks and circulates during the scene, offering drinks.

Wiggins And this can't be the view of the Congregationalist Church, Pastor Merrill.

Grandmother I want no arguments, Rector Wiggins.

Wiggins I'm not arguing, mam, I'm just a plain-speaking Episcopalian; my wife Barb will vouch for that.

Barb Oh, yes honey, I do I do – he flies a 'plane in exactly the same way.

Wiggins Either the Bible is true or it is not true.

Barb Straight from A to B, direct and to the point.

Wiggins A fact is a fact.

Merrill Well…it is my b-b-b-belief, and I speak for m-m-m-myself…

Wiggins For the children, sir.

Takes a refill off OWEN.

Thank you, son.

Merrill The Bible is a book with a troubling p-p-p-plot, but a p-plot that can be understood… God creates us out of love, but we don't want God, or we don't understand him, or we don't b-b-b-believe in him, or we pay very poor attention to him… Nevertheless, nevertheless –

God continues to love us – at least, he continues to try to get our attention…and the trick, the trick of having f-f-f-faith is that it is necessary to b-believe in God without any great or even remotely reassuring evidence that we don't inhabit a godless universe.

Wiggins But is the Bible true.

Merrill Let me p-p-p-put it another way, doubt is the cornerstone of our b-belief in God.

Wiggins What do you think, son.

Owen Belief is about faith not doubt, if you don't have that you're in the wrong business.

Wiggins That's right, son.

Takes another drink.

That's right.

Owen I know I'm right, and I'm not your son – sir.

Barb Such 'the little man'.

Wiggins How is your father.

Barb Such a charitable man, giving up his marshland like that so they could widen the river.

Owen It's not marshland, it's mud.

Wiggins We don't see much of him.

Owen Not many people do see my father, sir.

Lydia Circulate.

OWEN moves off.

Barb And you must be Lydia.

Lydia Yes.

Barb Mrs Wheelwright's companion.

Lydia No.

Barb Oh, I was told –

Lydia You were told wrong then. I'm the cook.

Barb The hors d'oeuvres are delicious.

Lydia I didn't cook them, I don't cook.

Barb But you're the cook.

Lydia I'm the cook.

Barb So what do you do.

Lydia I don't have any legs.

Barb Oh, I am sorry.

Merrill You are a very certain young man.

Owen I believe we are all here for a purpose.

Merrill But what do you do for fun, do you have fun.

John He likes being hung up on a peg and left in the dark.

Owen No, I don't.

John And he loves baseball, he collects baseball cards.

Merrill But you don't p-p-p-play.

Owen I play.

   MERRILL laughs.

   You don't believe me.

Merrill Oh, I believe you.

Owen We play Little League.

Lydia I did nothing to deserve this, I'm being punished, God's punishing me and I don't know for what.

Wiggins Our Lord moves in mysterious ways.

Lydia He should try moving in a wheelchair.

Owen We play next week, sir, you come and watch, they put me in to strike I'll hit a home run – you come and watch.

Merrill Yes.

Owen I will.

John He will.

Merrill Nothing in this life is for certain, Owen.

Owen That's for sure.

Merrill Yes, yes, of course – T-T-T-Tabitha.

Tabitha Yes, pastor.

Merrill Please, really there's no need to be so formal. Let me.

Takes tray off her. They exit.

Owen I don't like him.

John I like him. You don't like anyone.

Owen Yes I do, I like lots of people.

John Like who.

Owen Well…

John See, you don't.

Owen Groucho Marx and Mr Liberace.

Barb Mrs Wheelwright, I am so much enjoying your spread of aperitisers and hors d'oeuvres.

Grandmother Thank you.

Lydia Aperitifs.

Barb (*To LYDIA.*) I can only imagine what it feels like.

Lydia No, you can't.

Barb It's such a lovely house. Ours is wooden. I do so hope to live in a house with as much brick in it as yours one day. Don't we honey.

Wiggins Surely we do, Barb, surely we do. Barb always gets what she wants.

Barb I got you.

Wiggins You got me, alright.

Barb I got you.

Wiggins I was the airline pilot.

Barb And I was the stewardess.

Wiggins And you got me and I got God, I was flying on autopilot until I met Barb.

Lydia And what did God get.

Enter TABITHA.

Grandmother Oh, Tabitha – where's Pastor Merrill.

Tabitha On the phone to Mrs Merrill.

Grandmother Poor man.

Lydia But what did God get – you got Barb, Barb got you and you both got God, but what did God get.

Wiggins Two more souls for the Kingdom of Heaven.

Lydia Lucky God.

Enter MERRILL and pours himself a stiff drink.

Owen You look beautiful tonight, Miss Wheelwright.

Tabitha Tabitha.

Owen Tabitha.

Tabitha Why, thank you Owen. It's just an old sweater and skirt.

Owen You'd look beautiful in anything.

Grandmother How is Mrs Merrill.

Merrill Oh…b-b-b-better, much better…as well as can be expected considering the weather – and she so wanted to come, but one of the boys has come down with a t-t-t-temperature and she doesn't want to leave them…I offered to go but she insisted I stay – they seem to take after their mother, she's never got used to the climate.

Barb Where's she from.

Merrill California.

Lydia And she's the colour of an orange.

Merrill It's her natural colour.

Lydia She's got a sun lamp.

Merrill I should go.

Grandmother Nonsense, they'll call if they need you.

Merrill If you insist.

Grandmother I do. Have another drink.

Merrill Thank you.

Wiggins Of course for most people Christmas is the big event, but if you're in the business, if you're up in the cockpit holding the joystick and talking to air-traffic control – then it's Easter, Easter is the big one.

Grandmother (*To MERRILL.*) It breaks my heart, that she should become an Episcopalian.

Wiggins Easter, it's bigger than Christmas.

Grandmother I've said nothing, I'm saying nothing.

Merrill You do right.

Wiggins But you'll all come to our Nativity I hope – we always have a real baby, you can't fake the Lord Jesus – people know plastic when they see it.

Owen Another drink, rectum Wiggins.

Wiggins Thank you son, thank you.

Takes a drink.

Owen I'm not your son.

Barb Rector, Owen, Rector.

Owen That's what I said, what else would I say.

Barb Nothing, nothing honey.

Wiggins And young Owen here, he always plays our archangel.

Owen Not this year I'm not.

Barb You know all the words.

Owen I'm not doing it.

Wiggins Well who do you want to play, son.

Owen A non-speaking part.

The chimes of a soft dining bell.

Tabitha Listen everyone, listen to me please – I've got an announcement to make.

Lydia Oh, Lord preserve us all.

Silence.

Tabitha I met a man, a man on the Boston and Maine.

Silence.

Grandmother You mean another man.

Tabitha Yes, another man.

Grandmother Not 'that' man.

Tabitha No, not that man.

Wiggins What man.

Grandmother A man that you like.

Tabitha Yes, and I'm going to marry him.

Silence.

Barb Where did you meet him again, honey.

Tabitha On the train, on the Boston and Maine, just today – this morning in fact.

Barb And you're going to marry him.

Tabitha Yes.

Silence.

He's an Episcopalian.

Silence.

Merrill What about your singing lessons.

Tabitha What about them.

Merrill You'll continue with them.

Tabitha Why shouldn't I.

Merrill Well, I m-m-m-mean…

Grandmother What does this man do.

Tabitha Dramatics.

Wiggins An actor.

Lydia Lord have mercy.

Tabitha He teaches acting and putting on plays.

Wiggins A director.

Tabitha Not exactly.

Grandmother Tabitha.

Tabitha A teacher – he had an interview at the Academy today and that's how we met on the train. If they appoint him the first thing he's going to do is a production of a *A Christmas Carol*, I said you might be willing to volunteer your wheelchair, Lydia, for Tiny Tim. He went to Harvard – class of '45.

Grandmother Oh, a Harvard man, why didn't you say.

Tabitha I just did.

Grandmother Harvard, the class of '45, Lydia.

Lydia Yes, I heard.

Tabitha It's not important.

Lydia It all sounds like trouble to me.

Silence.

Barb My, my, what interesting lives you all do live.

Wiggins He's an Episcopalian.

Silence.

Lydia He's not a Cohen, or a Calamari, or a Meany, God forbid.

Tabitha No, he's a Needham.

Grandmother With a name like that they could have been on The Mayflower.

Tabitha He's called Dan.

Grandmother When are we going to meet him.

Tabitha I don't know.

Grandmother Where does he live.

Tabitha I don't know.

Grandmother Well, when will you see him.

Tabitha I don't know.

Grandmother And you're going to marry him.

Tabitha Yes.

Grandmother But you haven't made plans.

Tabitha No.

Grandmother Well, what if you never see him again.

Tabitha I will, I know I will.

Lydia You can't be such a know-it-all, Tabitha Wheelwright.

TABITHA looks at JOHN.

Tabitha It's alright Johnny, this man has no relationship whatsoever to the man who is your father – this is a man I saw for the first time today on the train and I like him, that's all, I just like him – and I think you'll like him too.

John Okay.

Doorbell rings.

Lydia Who's that.

Grandmother I don't know.

Lydia It'll be nobody decent – nobody decent calls round during Thanksgiving.

Tabitha No, no, you're wrong, Johnny – I'm not going to have a baby, I'm never going to have another baby, I have my baby – I'm just telling you that I've met a man. Someone I like. He's an Episcopalian, that's why we've become Episcopalians.

Merrill So, you didn't just meet him today.

Enter DAN NEEDHAM.

Dan They said I should come straight in.

Tabitha Everyone, this is Dan.

Dan Happy Thanksgiving.

Tabitha Dan, Grandma – Grandma, Dan.

Dan Pleased to meet you, mam.

Grandmother How tall are you.

Dan Six foot two.

Grandmother And you went to Harvard.

Dan Yes, mam.

Grandmother Where do you work.

Dan The Gravesend Academy for Boys. (*To TABITHA.*)
  I got the job.

Tabitha Isn't he just brilliant.

Merrill Brilliant.

Wiggins Congratulations, son.

  WIGGINS shakes DAN's hand.

  I expect we'll see you in church.

Dan Well –

Tabitha Rector Wiggins and his wife, Barb.

Barb It's a pleasure, a real pleasure to meet you, Dan.

Tabitha The Reverend Merrill.

Dan Sir.

Tabitha Owen Meany.

Dan Owen.

Tabitha Lydia.

Lydia Nobody decent.

Dan And John.

John How do you do, sir.

Dan Dan.

Gives JOHN a brown paper parcel.

John Thank you, sir.

Dan Dan. Open it now if you like.

Tabitha Open it, John.

John No, not now.

Dan You don't have to if you don't want to.

John Thank you, sir.

Dan Dan.

John Dan.

They shake hands.

TABITHA claps hands twice.

Tabitha Thanksgiving.

Owen Open it.

John What for.

Owen It's a present.

Tabitha Reverend Merrill, you sit at one end of the table and Rector Wiggins, you at the other, and we'll have two prayers.

John Probably just some stupid magic trick.

Owen I'd like a magic trick.

Exit GRANDMOTHER, LYDIA, WIGGINS and MERRILL. Strike table and chairs as they go.

Tabitha Oh, I'm so glad you could all make it – poor Mrs Merrill.

Barb Yes, poor Mrs Merrill.

BARB finishes drink in one. Exit BARB.

TABITHA takes DAN by arm.

Tabitha I do so love Thanksgiving.

She leads DAN out.

You can sleep over the night, Owen.

Owen Thanks Miss Wheelwright.

Tabitha Tabitha.

Owen Tabitha.

Exit TABITHA and DAN.

Open it.

JOHN opens the parcel. It's a brand new leather baseball glove.

John Gee.

Owen Wow.

John Smell it.

Owen Mmmh, yeah. Let me put it on, I want to put it on.

OWEN puts on glove.

John   What does it feel like.

Owen   Magic.

John   It's mine.

Owen   I love it.

OWEN raises hand with baseball above his head and looks up at it.

Music.

Set bed. TABITHA's flaming red dress on a tailor's dummy next to the bed. A telephone rings offstage. Set JOHN's bed. MR and MRS MEANY sitting.

Explosion. Dust. Scratch. Music stops.

Mr Meany   Damn phonograph.

Exit MR MEANY. Enter TABITHA chased by DAN.

Tabitha   No, no – Daniel Needham – don't you dare – leave off, stop, stop, stop it.

DAN catches her and they fall on bed centre stage.

Telephone stops ringing.

No, no, no.

He kisses her. They kiss.

Enter MR MEANY.

Mrs Meany   Who was that on the telephone.

Mr Meany   No one.

Mrs Meany   What did they want.

Mr Meany   Nothing.

Mrs Meany I worry, every time he goes out, I worry.

Mr Meany Well don't, I don't – it's got nothing to do with me.

Mrs Meany Don't say that, he's your son.

Mr Meany Is he.

Mrs Meany God will punish you.

Mr Meany He already has.

TABITHA sits up.

Tabitha No, you can't, you can't – not the night before. This is my bedroom.

Dan Where am I sleeping.

Tabitha Downstairs on the sofa. What sort of a girl do you think I am.

He kisses her.

Owen Your father is not your mother's singing teacher, that would be too obvious.

John Well he's the only realistic candidate we've got, at the moment.

Owen If it's him, why make it secret. It must be someone closer to home. I'm getting in the bed.

John No you're not.

Owen Yes, I am.

OWEN jumps on bed and they fight.

Mr Meany That was Owen. He's sleeping over.

Mrs Meany Again.

Mr Meany They don't mind.

Mrs Meany I worry.

Mr Meany So we're all happy then; he's happy not to be here, I'm happy that he's gone, and you ain't happy unless you're worrying. We're all happy.

Mrs Meany God will strike you dead.

Mr Meany Most days I wish He would.

Mrs Meany The night before her wedding day. That woman is an angel.

Mr Meany That's not a word I would use.

Mrs Meany You've got no soul.

Mr Meany I married you, didn't I.

OWEN pushes JOHN off bed.

Owen (*Jumping up and down.*) The winner.

John Cheat.

TABITHA pushes DAN off.

Tabitha Bed.

Dan Bed.

Tabitha Downstairs. You wouldn't respect me. Not the night before I get married.

Dan I might.

Tabitha No.

Dan I would, I do.

Tabitha Now. What sort of a girl do you think I am.

Dan My sort.

Tabitha It was meant, you were meant.

Dan You could wear that dress.

Tabitha No.

Dan I want to see you in that dress.

Tabitha You will. When we're married.

Dan Lucky me.

Tabitha Yes.

Dan I like it.

Tabitha I sleep with it by my bed always…

Dan I like your dress.

Tabitha Someone stood over, watching me in the dark –
John thought it was a man, a man in my bedroom once
and screamed the house down.

She laughs.

It was meant, you were meant, God sent you.

*Exit DAN. TABITHA undresses. Takes off clothes parallel
to OWEN and JOHN talking. OWEN in bed.*

Owen Your mother has the best breasts of all mothers.

John You really think so.

Owen Absolutely the best.

John What about Mrs Wiggins.

Owen Too big.

John Mrs Merrill.

Owen Very funny.

John Miss Judkins.

Owen I don't know. I can't remember them, but she's not a mother.

John Irene Babson.

Owen Don't give me the shivers. Your mother's the one. And she smells better than anyone else too.

TABITHA gets into bed. JOHN gets into bed with OWEN.

Dan really loves her. He loves her almost as much as we do.

John I know.

OWEN turns over. JOHN turns over the other way.

Owen I don't mind you know.

John You don't mind.

Owen No.

JOHN turns over.

Okay.

John Okay.

OWEN turns out the light.

Mrs Meany There's a storm brewing.

Owen Night, then.

John Night.

They go to sleep.

Mrs Meany A terrible frightening storm.

Mr Meany I'll fasten down the shutters.

Mrs Meany Like when Owen was born – the earth groaned, rivers swelled, stones and trees and woods were ripped up from the ground –

Mr Meany I seem to remember it rained.

Mrs Meany I had no one, I was alone.

Mr Meany The unspeakable outrage.

Exit MR MEANY.

Blackout. The storm outside. Strains of 'The Funeral March' and 'The Wedding March' come and go. Occassional flashes of lightning illuminate upstage as our heroes turn in their beds and MRS MEANY looks like Degas' 'Woman at the Window' with a flying hat on.

OWEN suddenly wakes and turns on a light.

Owen I feel sick.

John What, what is it.

Owen I feel sick.

John Are you going to puke.

Owen I don't know.

John What's that.

Owen It's the storm. I feel sick.

John Go and tell mom.

OWEN gets out of bed and goes. JOHN lies back and turns off light.

(*Shouts.*) No, Owen, wait – the dummy by mom's bed, it's just an old dummy –

Music. An ANGEL. OWEN transfixed as the ANGEL descends. OWEN lets out a blood-curdling wail. TABITHA wakes. Exit ANGEL. Music stops. Telephone rings.

Tabitha Owen, what is it.

Owen I saw an angel.

Tabitha No, Owen, it's just a stupid old dummy.

Telephone stops ringing. Lights up on MR and MRS MEANY.

Mr Meany That was Owen.

Mrs Meany Something bad has happened.

Mr Meany He's seen the angel of death hovering above Miss Wheelwright's bed. He's coming home.

Exit MR MEANY.

Enter GIRL ONE, MARY BETH and HAROLD with wooden Sunday school chairs, OWEN and JOHN. Exit MRS MEANY. Enter WIGGINS and BARB. CHILDREN settle down on chairs.

Barb Well, we all know who our descending angel is.

Owen Not me.

Barb Why, Owen.

Owen Put someone else up in the air. Maybe the shepherds can just look at a 'Pillar of Light' – the Bible says the Angel of the Lord appears to three shepherds, not to a whole congregation – and use someone with a voice that everyone doesn't laugh at.

All laugh.

Barb But Owen –

Wiggins No, no, Barb – if Owen's tired of being the angel we should respect his wishes, this is a democracy.

Owen And another thing: Joseph shouldn't smirk.

All laugh.

Barb Be quiet, children, this is the Lord's house.

Harold Okay, someone else do Joseph – I don't even like the guy, the guy's a jerk, all he does is stand around and watch, no wonder he smirks.

WIGGINS picks up a prayer book and throws it at HAROLD. Prayer book hits HAROLD's head.

Wiggins Now, let us cast the Nativity. I had no idea we'd suffered a smirking Joseph all these years.

OWEN raises hand.

Yes, Owen.

Owen Why do we have to have a turtledove.

Wiggins Honey, tell the boy why we have to have a turtledove.

Silence.

Mary Beth I've been a turtledove three times.

Barb Let's just hold on the turtledoves, what we need is an Angel.

Owen What about Joseph.

Barb We start with the Angel, it's tradition.

Wiggins Well, this year we can start with Joseph – we mustn't be frightened of change, honey. So, who will be our Joseph.

Silence.

OWEN puts up hand.

Yes, Owen.

Owen John, Johnny Wheelwright, sir – he's got the right countenance for it.

Wiggins Stand up, John.

JOHN stands.

Yes, I do believe he has. What do you think, Barb.

Barb That we always begin with the Angel – and here we are with a Joseph before a Mary and we don't have an Angel.

Wiggins Okay, okay – so, who wants to hang up in the air this year.

Silence.

Tell them about the view from up there, Owen.

Owen Well, sir…it's difficult.

Wiggins Tell them, son.

Owen Sometimes the harness cuts into your skin –

Wiggins Yes, but what about the view.

Owen Well, it's really dark up there – and there's lots of lines to remember –

Barb Yes we know, Owen, we know.

Owen It's not an easy part.

Wiggins Okay, we'll let Joseph pick Mary first, and then come back to the Angel.

OWEN raises hand.

Yes, Owen.

Owen Good idea, sir.

Wiggins Thank you, son.

BARB lets out a cry of exasperation.

Well, John, who do you want.

Silence.

Any girl you want, you can have her.

Silence.

Pick a girl, any girl that you want.

Owen Mary Beth, Mary Beth, sir, she's never been Mary – and that way Mary would be Mary.

Barb It's Joseph's choice, okay.

Owen Okay.

Barb Joseph chooses Mary.

Owen It was just a suggestion.

MARY puts hand in air.

Wiggins Mary.

Mary Beth Well…I know that I've only ever been a turtledove – but I really would like to be Mary.

Looks at GIRL ONE.

I've always wanted a brother, and I promise that I will love the baby Jesus.

Barb I want an Angel, and I want one now.

HAROLD shuts his eyes, folds his arms and tilts back on his chair.

Someone has to be the Angel.

HAROLD tilts too far back on his chair and crashes to the floor.

Wiggins Who was that.

Owen Harold Crosby, sir.

Wiggins Good for you, Harold.

Harold What. What.

Wiggins Now we have our Angel.

Harold But –

Owen He's afraid of heights, sir.

Wiggins Brave boy. What's next.

Girl One Did Mary Beth get the part of Mary, sir.

Wiggins She most certainly did, child.

MARY BETH lets out a squeal of delight.

(*To BARB.*) That's what happens when you embrace change, honey.

Mary Beth I will, I will, I will love that baby Jesus to pieces.

Wiggins Good for you, Mary. Well that seems to settle everything.

Owen There's one more thing.

Silence.

The Christ child.

Nods of approval from children.

Wiggins We always have a real live baby Jesus – and several waiting in the wings, in case of accidents or emergencies, it's tradition.

Barb We must all learn to embrace change, honey.

Wiggins I refuse to have a plastic Jesus.

Owen But all those babies, sir – just to get one to lie still in the manger without crying, and all the others cry offstage and you can hear them.

Barb You know a baby who won't cry, Owen.

Owen No – but I know someone small enough to look like a baby, old enough not to cry and who can fit in the crib.

Silence.

Mary Beth Owen, it's Owen, Owen's going to be my baby and I can pick him up.

Owen Well, if everyone wants me to do it, I suppose I could.

Cheering and clapping. Enter DAN.

Dan Damn amateurs.

Exit CHILDREN, WIGGINS and BARB. Enter LYDIA in wheelchair. DAN sets the stage for 'A Christmas Carol'.

Lydia Mind your tongue before the Lord and a lady.

Dan The mailman won't do it, the part isn't big enough, there aren't enough lines.

Lydia How many lines are there.

Dan None. It's a non-speaking part. If I don't get a Ghost of Christmas Yet to Come there will be no Christmas Carol, no Tiny Tim, no Bob Cratchet, no bah humbug, no Scrooge, nothing – and there's no coffee.

Lydia I got the last cup.

Dan (*Buries head in hands.*) Ohhhhhhh.

DAN sets chairs for audience.

Lydia What you need is someone that doesn't mind having a non-speaking role.

Dan Thanks, Lydia.

Lydia My pleasure. Who have you got playing Scrooge.

Dan Mr Fish.

Lydia Mr Fish.

Dan Yes.

Lydia Get too near him and you'll end up dead – first his wife, then his dog – he was all over me until I lost my legs, the man's an oil slick – and he doesn't go to church.

DAN and LYDIA sit.

Owen And it's another non-speaking part.

John The Ghost of Christmas Yet to Come.

Owen I auditioned before the whole company this morning.

John They didn't laugh.

Owen No, they didn't laugh – when I came on stage it was like they'd seen a real ghost – the Narrator fainted and Tiny Tim began yelling for his mom. They had no choice but to give me the part.

OWEN goes upstage. Enter GRANDMOTHER and TABITHA. Sit with DAN and LYDIA.

John God would tell me who my father was, Owen Meany had told me, but so far God had been silent and I remained sceptical. Now Owen was about to look into the future – but I didn't believe him, I never believed him until it was too late.

JOHN joins OWEN. Change into their nativity costumes.

Dan Something's not right. Small children burst into tears and don't make it to the happy ending. We've started warning mothers with small children at the door. It's not quite the family entertainment it's supposed to be. Kids leave the theatre like they've seen Dracula.

Grandmother Surely, something can be done about that boy's voice – medically speaking, that is, Daniel.

Dan But it's a non-speaking part.

Lydia That boy's voice comes straight from hell, it's the voice of the Devil.

Grandmother Lydia.

Exit DAN.

OWEN in swaddling clothes reading a newspaper. JOHN dressed as Joseph.

Owen 'Little'.

John You stole the show.

Owen 'Diminutive'.

John They don't even mention Scrooge and he's the lead – how do you think Mr Fish feels.

Owen Do they say, 'Suspected wife-killer, suspected dog-killer, avowed atheist Mr Fish'. What's my height got to do with it.

JOHN takes newspaper.

John 'A star… Brilliant… Huge presence' – what more do you want.

Owen They call me 'Diminutive'.

John You forgot 'Tiny Tim-sized'.

Enter MR FISH.

Fish I just wanted to say good luck.

Owen Mister Fish.

Fish And to congratulate you on your notices for *A Christmas Carol.*

John Oh, yes.

Owen You're not a churchgoer, Mr Fish.

Fish Why no, I'm not, just weddings and funerals, but I wouldn't miss this for the world. How much of the story does it cover – I have to leave at the intermission to prepare for Scrooge.

John There is no intermission.

Fish I don't want to miss the bit where they stick a crown of thorns on your head.

Owen It's not the whole thing you know.

Fish Not the bit on the cross.

Owen No. They didn't nail him to the cross when he was a baby.

Fish Oh, dear, that's a pity – I'll probably just watch her give birth and then go.

Enter DAN.

My, my, look who's here.

Dan Mr Fish.

Fish I'd better go, I'll see you later, on stage – break a leg.

Exit MR FISH.

Lydia If I have to leave I will leave.

Grandmother Suck on a mint and stop complaining.

Lydia I don't complain, I make statements of fact.

Grandmother You complain.

JOHN takes up position ready for Nativity.

Owen You've seen the reviews for *A Christmas Carol.*

Dan Maybe you'd like to invite your parents.

Owen No.

Dan Tonight's the last show.

Owen You don't run away to the circus, Dan, so your family can come too.

Dan But surely –

Owen No. They won't like it, they don't like anything make-believe, they're realists – and anything with ghosts is out – they only like true stories.

Dan Whatever you say.

Owen I do. Now if you don't mind, Dan, I need a few moments on my own in order to prepare for the Virgin Birth.

Dan How do you do that.

Owen By thinking of where Our Lord has just come from.

Dan The Virgin Mary.

Owen The kingdom of Heaven, Dan, the kingdom of Heaven.

Exit DAN. Goes back to his seat. TABITHA waves at someone in audience.

Grandmother Who are you waving at.

Tabitha No one.

Lydia Even if it means walking across the stage, I'll walk out.

DAN sits next to TABITHA.

Tabitha Look, there's the Reverend Merrill.

Lydia And his luckless wife.

GRANDMOTHER waves.

That woman uses a sun lamp.

Grandmother Lydia.

Enter MR and MRS MEANY. They take their seats.

I thought the Meanys weren't coming.

Tabitha No, that's Scrooge, ma – they won't go and see Scrooge on account of the fact that it's a made-up story, they only like true stories.

Dan Such as the Nativity.

Lydia Please tell your husband that if we are to remain on cordial speaking terms it would be better if he remained silent.

Enter MR FISH, who takes his seat on the Christmas Carol set as Scrooge.

Mrs Meany I don't think we should have come.

Mr Meany Nonsense, he's your son.

Mrs Meany It's blasphemy.

Mr Meany It's a comedy, God's comedy.

Enter MARY BETH, BOY ONE, HAROLD and GIRL ONE.

The Nativity is set.

Dan Owen's running a fever.

Lydia Shhh.

Dan He's got this and then Scrooge – I don't know, I just don't know.

Lights dim. The manger bathed in light. Music: 'Away in a Manger', played on recorders.

OWEN steps into the light and takes his place in the manger.

Lydia Be quiet sir, Our Lord is born.

Lights up on Scrooge in chair.

Fish If I could work my will every idiot who goes about with 'Merry Christmas' on his lips should be boiled with his own pudding, and buried with a stake of holly through his heart. Bah – humbug.

Enter BARB WIGGINS. She goes over to OWEN in manger.

Enter WIGGINS. Straps HAROLD into harness and winches him up.

Barb I just wanted to say good luck.

She kisses him full on the lips. OWEN struggles to break free. BARB goes to operate hoist for descending angel. A pillar of light appears over the manger. The Christ child sneezes. 'O Little Town of Bethlehem.' HAROLD descends haltingly in the pillar of light. MARY BETH as Mary offers the Christ child a hanky.

Harold Be not afraid…

Mary Beth Blow.

Boy One (*A shepherd standing at the manger whispers off.*) The Christ child's got a boner.

Voice (*Off.*) Say again.

The Angel halts suddenly.

Harold Be not afraid…

Boy One (*Whispers louder.*) The Christ child's got a hard on.

Voice (*Off.*) I can't hear you.

Mary Beth Why won't you blow.

Boy One (*Loud.*) Jesus has got an erection.

The angel suddenly ascends haltingly out of sight.

Harold Be not very afraid…

HAROLD flies out. Scrooge on his knees. Praying hard.

Fish Oh, cold, cold, Bah-Humbug, rigid, dreadful Death, set up thine altar here, let me see my future – O Spirit, remove me from this place.

OWEN sits up shaking with anger.

Owen (*Shouts.*) What are you doing here… You shouldn't be here… (*Points at MEANYS.*) It's a sacrilege for you to be here…

MR MEANY stands.

Mr Meany (*To audience.*) It's his mom, she just wanted to see her son act.

Owen It's an unspeakable outrage.

Mr Meany This place ain't fit for decent people.

Exit MR MEANY.

Exit MARY BETH, BOY ONE and GIRL ONE.

Fish (*As Scrooge, on knees, arms outstretched, looking up to Heaven.*) Come for me, Spirit, Spirit of Christmas Yet to Come, and show me my future, take me. Bah-Humbug.

OWEN pulls swaddling blanket over his head like a hood and is completely cloaked from head to foot. OWEN's hand emerges from the cloak, beckons MR FISH forward and points to a gravestone.

Before I draw nearer to that stone, answer me one question. Are these the shadows of what Will be or are they shadows of things that May be, only.

Silence.

OWEN is drawn magnetically to the gravestone.

Wait for me, spirit…

FISH follows OWEN. OWEN stands over over gravestone mumbling.

Tell me whose name it is you see…tell me…tell me Owen.

OWEN remains standing over gravestone mumbling to himself.

It was the best of times, it was the worst of times… (*Looks at OWEN and away again.*) Fog, fog, fog – fog everywhere, fog down the river, fog on the Essex Marshes – (*To OWEN.*) What is it Owen… (*Away.*) fog in the eyes and throats of Greenwich pensioners, fog, fog, fog… fog… (*To OWEN.*) What's the matter, Owen… (*Away.*) Gotta pick a pocket or two, boys, you gotta pick a pocket or two –

OWEN slips the blanket back off his head, turns and looks eyes streaming with tears, at MR FISH. Then points at gravestone. Turns back to look at it and lets out a shrill, piercing, blood-curdling yell.

The name of OWEN MEANY appears on gravestone. 'First Lt. Paul Owen Meany Jr.' The date of death underneath. Indecipherable. Pool of light on OWEN on floor in JOHN's arms.

Owen It was my name on the grave.

John No, you made a mistake.

Owen It was my name, not Ebeneezer Scrooge…my name in full.

John You're not well, you've got a fever.

Owen No…it was a vision – I saw my own grave, I know when I'm going to die. God has shown me when I am going to die.

End of Act One.

ACT TWO

Enter JOHN. Baseball game. JOHN, OWEN, BOY ONE and COACH CHICKERING on the bench.

John Baseball is boring.

Roar of crowd.

I don't know when I bat.

Owen I know when you bat. If Harold gets on, I'm on deck – if Buzzy gets on, I'm up.

John Fat chance – is there only one out.

Owen Two out.

Chickering Buzzy's on first, Owen you're up.

OWEN stands with bat.

Chickering Swing away kid, swing away.

Boy One Knock the cover off the ball, Meany.

OWEN takes up position centre stage, ready to hit.

John Give it a ride, Owen.

Chickering Hit away kid, hit away.

OWEN limbers up. Stands ready to strike. Remains still. Turns head and watches ball fly past him.

Voice (*Off.*) Strike one.

Chickering Swing, I said, swing.

Owen That was too far away.

OWEN limbers up for second strike. Stands ready for pitch.
OWEN drops bat and dives to the ground head first. Everyone
on the bench laughs.

Voice (*Off.*) Strike two.

OWEN stands and cleans himself off and prepares for the
third pitch. Enter TABITHA. Searches bleachers for someone.
OWEN pulls bat back and swings. As baseball bat comes
forward, a loud sharp crack. OWEN drops bat and watches
trajectory of the departing ball. JOHN, CHICKERING
and rest of bench stand and also watch the ball. At same
time TABITHA waves to someone in the bleachers. Blackout
on all but for a spotlight on TABITHA waving. Repeat of
loud sharp crack of baseball bat.

Blackout. Collective gasp from crowd.

Silence.

Lights up. TABITHA dead on ground.

Silence.

Owen I'm sorry.

Silence.

Exit OWEN. COACH CHICKERING and CHIEF PIKE
at body.

Chickering No Johnny, no Johnny. You don't want to see
her, Johnny.

Pike Where's the ball.

Chickering The ball, you want the fucking ball.

Pike Well, it's the murder weapon.

Chickering The murder weapon.

Pike The instrument of death, I guess you'd call it.

Chickering The fucking murder weapon, Jesus Christ, Ben – it was a baseball.

Pike Well, where is it. If it killed somebody, I'm supposed to see it – actually I'm supposed to possess it.

Chickering Don't be an asshole, Ben.

Pike Did one of your kids take it.

Chickering Ask them – don't ask me.

John (*Shouts.*) Owen!

Boy One He went home.

Harold He had his bike.

John Owen!

Pike Who's got the ball.

Chickering Asshole.

Pike That goddam Meany kid's got the ball.

Chickering In hell's name, Ben.

Pike Evidence, Ted, evidence.

PIKE goes to leave.

Chickering Where you going, Ben.

Pike Biscuits and gravy, Ted, death makes me hungry – I'm buying.

Chickering But we can't just leave her, Ben.

Pike Why not.

Chickering It ain't decent.

Pike She ain't going nowhere. She's already got where she's going. God's punishment for that boy of hers.

Exit PIKE. Exit CHICKERING. JOHN alone on stage.

John Owen.

A fusion of 'The Funeral March' and 'The Wedding March' plays. Enter DAN. TABITHA takes his hand and they walk as if up the aisle. Set long table with white tablecloth. At one end silver chalice of wine and MERRILL. At the other, silver platter of communion wafers and WIGGINS.

No, no.

TABITHA and DAN stand before table as at an altar.

This isn't happening, you're not here, you're always here – this isn't real –

WIGGINS blesses the bread. MERRILL blesses the wine. Enter congregation, all in black. Includes all key players.

She's dead, she died, there was nothing I could do, she never got to tell me who my real father was. I was eleven years old.

Wiggins The Lord is my shepherd, I shall not be in want.

John Where was the Lord when I needed him.

Enter OWEN and MR MEANY. They stand apart from the congregation.

No.

Merrill Yea.

John No.

Merrill Yea, though I walk through the valley of the shadow of death, I will fear no evil, for you are with me; your rod and your staff, they comfort me.

67

John My name is John Wheelwright – I am forty-five years old – I live in Canada –

Wiggins Daniel Needham, wilt thou have this woman to thy wedded wife.

Dan I will.

John No.

Wiggins Tabitha Wheelwright, wilt thou have this man to thy wedded husband.

John No, this isn't happening.

MERRILL gives ring to DAN. DAN slips ring on TABITHA's finger. He lifts TABITHA's veil. They kiss. DAN lifts TABITHA's body onto the table and lays it out.

You died, God died, and nothing was certain.

Owen God has taken your mother. My hands were the instrument. God has taken my hands. I am God's instrument. It's the will of God – these hands, this body, my soul, my voice, it's all for God, for a purpose.

Merrill Help us, we pray, in the midst of things we cannot understand.

John I couldn't pray.

Owen Faith and prayer, John, faith and prayer – they work, they really do.

Exit TABITHA and DAN to hymn. 'Crown Him with Many Thorns', followed by congregation. Exit MR MEANY in opposite direction. Exit WIGGINS and MERRILL.

John God doesn't care – God punishes – God gives and God takes… and demands love, demands faith, blind faith, blind obedience, down on our knees with our hands clasped tight, castrated and impotent before the living God – some light in the cold empty dark, something to cling on to, some hope, and I look, and I cling on to myself, and there's no one, nobody, only me… God took everything.

Owen I was God's instrument.

John Fuck God.

Owen I won't let you die, Johnny.

Three loud cracks of the baseball bat. Exit OWEN.

John 'I won't let you die.' Did you say that, did he really say that. I don't remember him saying that, 'I won't let you die John.'

Enter DAN with box. DAN puts box down.

Dan It came this morning.

Silence.

I'll leave you to open it.

John I don't want it.

Dan He loved you.

John No.

Dan It's his gift. I'm here if you need me.

Exit DAN.

JOHN goes to box.

John (*Reads.*) Owen Meany: Diaries 1960 to 1968.

Opens box. Takes out a diary. Opens diary and reads.

(*Reads.*) This diary was given to me for Christmas 1960 by my benefactor Mrs Harriet Wheelwright –

Enter OWEN.

Owen Your grandmother's getting a television.

John Good.

Owen Now we can watch Liberace live.

John You and my grandmother.

Owen Yeah.

Enter GRANDMOTHER.

Grandmother Mr Liberace is a gentleman.

Owen He wouldn't hurt anyone.

Grandmother He actually likes old people.

Owen He gave his brother a job and he's not especially talented.

Grandmother He loves his mother.

John What about all those jewels and that silly hair and the ridiculous costumes.

Owen/Grandmother (*Together.*) Oh, we love them.

Grandmother It's not serious.

Owen It's showbusiness.

Grandmother And he has publicly declared, from the witness box, his opposition to all forms of homosexuality.

John Oh, that's alright then – one of the good guys.

Owen Don't knock your grandma.

John So, now you're pals.

Grandmother/Owen (*Together.*) We've always been pals.

John You don't like the television, it drains people of life, remember.

Grandmother So did Lydia, but we never got rid of her.

John She died.

Grandmother Television is my hobby.

John And you, if you're so smart, how can you like Liberace at your age – you might only be five foot tall, look ten years old and speak like Mickey Mouse – but you're sixteen, you smoke a pack of Camels every day and you just got your driver's licence.

Owen You expected me to fail.

John How did you get your feet to touch the pedals.

Owen I tied wooden blocks to them.

Enter DAN.

Dan Owen likes Liberace because Liberace couldn't exist in Gravesend; in Liberace, Owen has found an exotic and culturally acceptable expression of 'difference' through which he can displace his own anxieties.

John No, Dan, he likes the songs.

Dan Liberace is a safety valve through which Owen can let off steam.

John Let off steam, he thinks that his voice comes direct from God, he thinks that he is God's instrument.

Dan We all have to look out for Owen, and pray that madness doesn't run in the family.

Exit GRANDMOTHER. Bent rusted basketball hoop. Basketball thrown to JOHN. JOHN throws ball to OWEN and stands under hoop. OWEN dribbles ball.

Owen JFK – JFK – JFK all the way.

Enter BOY ONE, HAROLD and MARY BETH. Playing game of basketball.

Exit DAN.

Boy One Slam-dunk Meany.

Harold Make way for the slam-dunk master.

Boy One 'Stuff' the ball, kid.

OWEN throws ball to JOHN and runs at speed towards him. JOHN throws the ball up above the net. OWEN leaps into JOHN's waiting arms. JOHN boosts OWEN above the basket's rim, OWEN stuffs the ball. Clapping, whistling and cheering.

Owen JFK – JFK – JFK all the way.

John Meanwhile, in South East Asia the French were taking their leave and in the Pentagon they heard the drums of war. But right then our draft cards meant nothing, we kept them in our back pockets; forged birthdates, fake ID for buying liquor with, Owen's idea. No one had even heard of Vietnam.

Owen And again.

John No.

Owen We need to get the timing of this leap right so you can lift me higher.

John What for.

Boy One Impressive, Meany. I'm impressed. I may even
consider using you in a game.

Owen It's not for a game.

Mary Beth What's showing at the Idaho.

Owen Another male-nipple movie.

Boy One *The Ten Commandments*.

Mary Beth Oh.

Owen *The Ten Commandments* and it's nearly Easter. All
that Old Testament rubbish when we should be thinking
of Jesus and the resurrection.

Mary Beth I like James Dean.

Harold What about Natalie Wood.

Boy One It's only a movie, nobody believes in that
religious shit anymore.

Owen Asshole.

Boy One What did you just call me.

Owen Asshole, I called you an asshole – asshole.

Boy One Hit me.

Harold Yeah, go on, hit him.

Owen What for.

Boy One Why not.

Owen I don't believe in it, I don't believe in fighting.

Harold He doesn't believe in fighting.

Boy One What do you believe in.

Owen God.

Harold He believes in God.

Boy One Come on, leave him alone.

Harold You what.

Boy One I said leave him.

> *Exit BOY ONE, HAROLD and MARY BETH. Enter TABITHA and DAN.*

Tabitha No, Daniel, no, no, leave me alone…

> *They kiss.*

John If my mother was still alive she'd be forty-five today.

> *Exit DAN.*

Owen And still beautiful.

John Every day I remember the crowd in that baseball stand and try to see him.

Owen Who.

John The man she was waving at, my father.

Owen You don't know that.

John I know it.

Owen Stop looking. She was a good mother. If she thought the guy could be a good father to you, you'd already know him.

John You're so damn smart.

Owen I'm just warning you; it's exciting looking for your father but don't expect to be too thrilled when you find

74

him. Everytime you get a boner, try to think if you remind yourself of anyone you know.

Transformation of TABITHA into a statue of Mary Magdalene.

Prostitute.

John What.

Owen She's a prostitute. It's a fucking joke. Mary Magdalene. The statue of a prostitute outside of a school run by nuns.

OWEN spits at the statue.

John Don't do that.

Owen Catholics. Let's just practice the shot, okay.

John Okay.

OWEN picks up basketball and dribbles. JOHN lights cigarette.

Owen Are you practicing or not.

John What for.

Owen Because I need you to.

John My feet hurt, my ankles are swollen and I'm thirsty.

Owen How do you think Christ felt up on the cross.

John I'm not Jesus.

Owen No, and all I'm asking you to do is practice a basketball shot.

John It's pointless.

Owen It's not pointless, nothing is pointless – everything has a purpose, you dumb-shit motherfucking asshole.

Enter a NUN. She walks across stage.

John Sister.

Owen Sister.

Exit NUN and TABITHA.

Fucking penguins. It's unnatural. They're unnatural. I'm going to get laid every night of my life.

John Yeah.

OWEN throws basketball to JOHN.

My feet hurt.

Owen So take off your shoes.

John No.

Owen Stop complaining then.

John Okay, okay – one more go.

JOHN throws ball to OWEN.

Owen Ready.

John Ready.

OWEN bounces ball on the spot hard, throws it to JOHN and runs at him.

Owen –

OWEN stops.

Owen Now what.

John I feel guilty every time I get an erection.

Exit OWEN.

Exit JOHN.

Front room of GRANDMOTHER's house. Enter RANDY WHITE, SAM WHITE, GRANDMOTHER, LYDIA standing next to plate of cookies on occasional table in centre of room.

White My wife and I both come from 'meat family' backgrounds in the Chicago area.

Sam But there's more money in the meat I come from.

White I worked in the family slaughterhouse, but finally, education drew me away from meat – it's the future mam, and what could be more important than that.

Sam A good steak.

White My wife has a very fine sense of humour.

Grandmother Have another cookie.

White With pleasure.

He takes a cookie.

Sam I couldn't help but notice a wheelchair in the hall.

Grandmother A friend's.

Sam Where is she.

Grandmother She died.

Exit LYDIA.

Silence.

Sam I hear there's been a lot of death in your family.

White Gravesend is very much to our liking. It's such a relief to be amongst one's own. To be able to walk down the street and feel that you belong, to not feel swamped by alien ways of life. Your family came over with the Founding Fathers.

Grandmother To escape persecution.

White Intolerable.

Sam It must have been a pain hard to bear, to have lost a
daughter at such a young age.

Silence.

Grandmother I made the cookies myself.

Silence.

White I have always maintained that the three most
important men in history are Jesus Christ, Adolf Hitler
and Carl Gustav Jung. Good and evil, reverse sides of
the same coin; Christ and the anti-Christ, and the
'collective unconscious'. I keep all their pictures hung
on my study wall.

Sam My husband believes in the 'unconscious'.

White God and the unconscious.

Leans toward cookies.

May I.

Helps himself.

Education, education, education. The future of
Gravesend Academy is safe in my hands as headmaster.
Hard work will be rewarded, slackness and indolence
penalised, a meritocracy of learning. And to begin with
I fully intend to abolish Latin.

Enter OWEN with a large copy of the Voice, student newspaper.

Owen (*Reads.*) So, the new headmaster has abolished Latin.
Hurrah! And what could be more popular with students
than abolishing a requirement. But should this have

been a unilateral decision taken by the headmaster alone. Surely this should have been accomplished by a vote – in faculty meeting. Is this decision actually legal. Are we descending into a form of school government in which the power is vested in a few persons or in a dominant class or clique; in short an oligarchy, government of the many by the few.

White So you're a Democrat, Meany.

Owen Yes sir. It'll be nice to have a president who people under thirty don't laugh at.

White I appreciate your 'vigah', young man, but let there be no misunderstanding: I am a Republican, an Illinois Republican.

Owen Good for you, sir.

White And as you boys know Illinois is the land of Lincoln.

Owen Illinois is the land of Adlai Stevenson and he's still alive.

White Mr Nixon may not seem glamorous to you –

Owen No sir, he's downright ugly.

White But this election wasn't a beauty contest or a sailing race, it's blood and guts politics – and the country will pay dearly for electing this Catholic patsy.

Owen I don't care if he is a mackerel snapper, he's got something we need –

White He's got nothing I need.

Owen The very thing Isaiah had in mind –

White Don't get smart with me, son.

Owen 'The people who walked in darkness have seen a great light; those who dwelt in a land of deep darkness, on them has light shined. For to us a child is born, to us a son is given; and the government will be upon his shoulder.' Remember.

White John F Kennedy was not what Isaiah had in mind.

Owen Ask not what your country can do for you – ask what you can do for your country.

White I think it's time you saw the school psychiatrist.

Exit RANDY WHITE, GRANDMOTHER and SAM WHITE.

JOHN throws the basketball at OWEN.

John You didn't tell me about the dream.

Owen Let's just practice the shot, okay.

John Okay.

As OWEN speaks, the numbers on a scorer's clock upstage and above them light up brightly with 00:04.

JOHN standing underneath a basketball hoop.

Ready.

Owen We have just four seconds.

John Yeah.

Owen Go.

On this word the clock counts down. OWEN throws ball to JOHN. OWEN runs at speed to JOHN. JOHN throws ball up above the net. OWEN jumps into JOHN's hands. JOHN lifts OWEN up into the air. OWEN stuffs basketball through hoop. As the ball drops into the net, OWEN shouts.

Time.

The clock stops at 00:01.

Silence. JOHN and OWEN stare at clock.

You see what a little faith can do. (*Shouts off.*) Set the clock to three.

John That's impossible, we'll never do it under three.

Owen If we can do it under four then we can do it under three, it just takes a little more faith.

John It takes more practice.

Owen (*Shrill.*) Faith takes practice.

John Do you think your voice will ever change.

Owen No, and I don't want it to change.

John You could have surgery.

Owen I don't want surgery. It's for a purpose.

John Sorry I forgot, God's instrument.

Owen Yeah, that's right.

John And God's going to tell me who my father is.

Owen Yes.

John I'm still waiting.

Enter BOY ONE and LARRY LISH with wooden prayer chairs. Set them for next scene and sit. OWEN sits. Enter MERRILL. JOHN sits. Divinity class, Gravesend Academy for Boys.

Merrill Doubt is the essence of, not the opposite of faith. The secret of faith is belief without miracles. A faith that needs a miracle is no faith at all – don't ask for proof.

John But everyone needs a little proof.

Merrill Faith itself is a miracle.

Boy One You can say that again, sir.

Merrill Y-y-y-yes I will. The first miracle I believe in is my own f-f-faith itself. We are born we die, nothing else in this world is certain.

John That's for sure.

Owen You don't believe in fate then.

Merrill It's hard not to b-b-believe in fate with the b-b-b-benefit of hindsight – the trick is to b-b-believe in fate with f-f-f-foresight.

Owen Fate isn't a magic trick, and it isn't something you look, or even ask for, it just happens.

Merrill We all f-f-f-find God within ourselves.

Owen You invent God through yourself.

Merrill No, I find Him and ask for His love.

Owen No, the point is God doesn't love us because we ask Him or because we're smart or good. We're stupid and we're bad and God loves us anyway.

Larry There's hope for us yet.

Owen Jesus kept on telling those dumb-shit disciples what was going to happen, 'The son of man will be delivered into the hands of men, and they will kill him.' That's in Mark, right.

Merrill Yes, but let's not say dumb-shit disciples.

Owen But you see my point.

Merrill Not quite.

Owen A bunch of assholes and God still loved them. Hell, Jesus even tells Peter that he's going to deny him three times before the cock crows – and what does the dumb-shit go and do – cockadoodle-do, whoops me and my big mouth – and God entrusts the little shit with founding the Catholic Church, no wonder it's all gone horribly wrong.

Merrill Thank you, Owen.

Owen And he's on the gate.

Merrill Thank you.

Owen What does that say. God's put a simpleton on the gate. He wants as many people to come in as possible, He loves us all no matter what – all it takes is faith, not blind faith, faith.

Exit MERRILL. LARRY LISH lights up a joint.

John President Kennedy has said that US advisers in Vietnam will return fire if fired upon.

Larry School's a drag.

Owen I hope we're advising the right guys.

Larry A real drag. Where is Vietnam.

John The guy we're advising is a Vietnamese Catholic.

Owen What's a Catholic doing in charge of a Buddhist country.

Larry President Kennedy is diddling with Marilyn Monroe.

Owen That is a truly tasteless lie.

Larry It's true, my mother told me. Ask her for yourself, she's down for my exeat.

John That's nice.

Larry She's a joke.

Owen How does your mother know.

Larry She knows all the Kennedys.

Owen You're disgusting.

Larry The world's disgusting.

Owen You're lying.

Larry My mother's a gossip, my mother's a bitch, but she's not a liar; she doesn't have the imagination to make anything up.

Enter MRS LISH. Exit BOY ONE with joint.

Larry darling.

She proffers her cheek.

You're still my baby.

You're embarrassing Owen and John.

Owen No you're not.

John No no, really you're not.

LARRY kisses his mother on the cheek.

Owen Hello Mrs Lish, nice to see you again.

Lish Oh I remember you, you're the boy with the funny voice.

Owen Yes that's me alright. How's the divorce going.

Larry Go on, tell them, tell them mom, tell them what you know about the President fooling around, they don't believe me.

Lish It's not 'mom' Larry, I'm not your mom.

Owen It must be very painful for you, Mrs Lish.

Lish It is, such vulgar vocabulary.

Owen To have to fight for custody of your only son.

Lish You want to know about the President, I'll tell you about the President – not only does he fool around with Marilyn Monroe but with countless others too.

Owen Does Jackie know.

Lish She must be used to it by now. What do you think of that.

Owen I think it's wrong.

Lish (*To LARRY.*) Is he for real.

Larry Isn't he a classic.

Owen It's a disgrace.

Lish Tell me something, boy, if Marilyn Monroe wanted to sleep with you, would you let her. Well.

Owen No – not if I were the President and certainly not if I was married.

Lish Are you kidding me.

Owen No, I am not.

John No, he isn't.

Larry No, he's for real.

Lish This is the future.

Larry Sure is, mom.

Lish This is the head of the class of the country's most prestigious fucking school and this is what we can expect of our future leaders – and don't call me mom. I'm not your fucking mom. I'm your mother.

Owen Of course I'm not the President and I'm not married and I don't know Marilyn Monroe and she probably wouldn't even want to sleep with me – but you know what, if you wanted to sleep with me – I mean right now, when I'm not the President and I'm not married – what the hell, let's give it a go.

Lish What did you just say to me.

Owen Come on, Mrs Lish.

Lish I am a personal friend of Billy Graham's.

Owen Fuck me, Mrs Lish.

Portrait of Carl Jung flown in centre stage, portraits of Adolf Hitler and Jesus Christ flown in on either side and lower down.

Exit MRS LISH and LARRY.

Enter WHITE, MERRILL, DAN, DR DOLDER and SAM WHITE.

It was a joke. She made it clear that she thought I was a joke and so I responded appropriately.

Sam You thought it appropriate to proposition a fellow student's mother.

White It's alright dear, I can handle this. (*Stern.*) And on school property.

Sam It's grounds for dismissal.

Merrill L-L-L-Let us not be hasty in our judgement, 'Let he who cast the first stone be without sin.'

Dolder May I ask a question, Headmaster.

White By all means, Professor.

Sam This boy needs thrashing, not psychoanalysing.

Dolder It's alright Owen, nobody wants to punish you – we just want to find out what happened, to understand what's going on, so that we can put it right.

Sam Oh, really.

John Mrs Lish laughed at Owen, she laughed in his face…she bullied him.

Owen She was sexy with me.

Dolder I see.

Sam The boy is evil, it's that simple.

Owen Mrs Lish revealed to me some particularly damning and unpleasant gossip.

Dolder What is this gossip.

Silence.

John Owen.

Owen No.

John Tell them.

Owen It's confidential information – (*Aside to JOHN*.)
  think of the scandal, what would happen to the President
  if such a rumour leaked to the newspapers.

Dolder What rumour.

White Speak, son, or I'll have no choice but to eject you
  from this school.

Dan You can't – it would serve no good purpose, it would
  ruin Owen's chances of a scholarship to Harvard or Yale
  – Owen is the brightest student this school's ever had –
  think of the boy.

White Speak, son.

  Silence.

John Do you want to get kicked out of school for
  protecting someone who doesn't even know you.

Owen (*To JOHN*.) He's the President, he's more important
  than I am, it's a threat to national security. I can say no
  more.

Sam There is no excuse, there can be no excuse – you
  crudely propositioned Mrs Lish in front of her son – I
  repeat 'crudely' – you were insulting, you were lewd,
  you were obscene – and you were anti-Semitic.

Owen Is Mrs Lish Jewish. I didn't know she was Jewish.

Sam She says you were anti-Semitic.

Owen Because I propositioned her.

Sam So you admit you 'propositioned' her – beat him and
  throw him out.

Dan No – put Owen on disciplinary probation, that's punishment enough, more than enough.

Merrill And if I may suggest, some p-p-p-pastoral tuition in my office once a week for a term.

Dolder (*Looking at MERRILL.*) And twice a week in my office, for one hour, for a year.

Portraits of HITLER, JUNG and JESUS flown out. Exit DAN, WHITE and SAM. MERRILL and DOLDER sit in swivel chairs on opposite sides of the stage.

OWEN centre stage.

Owen Father forgive them; for they know not what they do.

John What do you talk about to Dr Dolder.

Dolder So you are attracted to older women.

Owen No I'm not.

Dolder Why are you attracted to older women.

Owen I'm not.

Dolder You love the woman you killed with a baseball.

Owen Yes.

Dolder You loved her yet you killed her, why is that.

Owen It was God, I am God's instrument.

Dolder So you believe in God.

Owen Yes.

Dolder I see.

John (*To OWEN.*) But what do you tell him.

Owen The truth. I answer every question he asks truthfully and without humour.

John You tell him everything you think about and everything you believe. Not everything you believe.

Pause.

Right.

Owen Wrong. Everything, everything he asks.

John And what do you talk to Pastor Merrill about.

Merrill Oh – oh – I see you got here early.

Owen Yes, I was just looking at your desk.

Merrill Sit down, sit down.

Owen I like your office. What do you keep in the desk.

Merrill Nothing.

Owen You must keep something in it, all those drawers.

Merrill Nothing.

Owen So why is it locked.

Merrill I-I-I-I lost the key.

Owen Oh.

Merrill You looked in the top right hand drawer.

Owen Why not.

Silence.

Merrill So what do you want to talk about.

Owen The resurrection: 'woe unto them that call evil good and good evil.'

Merrill I see.

John What do you talk to Merrill about.

Owen Life after death.

Dolder I see.

Merrill I see.

John I see. (*To self.*) But I didn't, I didn't see, I didn't realise the degree to which Owen Meany never got tired of talking about death.

Owen (*Looking out front.*) I know when I'm going to die.

Dolder How do you know this.

Owen I've seen my gravestone.

Merrill You had a fever.

Owen It was a vision.

Dolder Was it.

Owen Yes it was.

Merrill You were hallucinating.

Dolder And when are you going to die.

Owen The thirty-first of March 1968.

Merrill It wasn't real.

Owen It was real, it's real I'm going to die on the thirty-first March 1968 at eleven o'clock in the morning – and I know how I'm going to die.

Dolder How do you know.

Owen I had a dream.

Dolder I see.

Merrill I see.

Owen A terrible, frightening dream.

Merrill It didn't mean anything, it was just a dream.

Owen I saw my own death.

> *OWEN rises into the air. Sound of helicopters.*

I was high up in the air and there were palm trees down below and I saw myself die.

> *OWEN ascending.*

And helicopters.

Dolder What do you think this means.

Owen I'm going to die in a hot country.

Merrill It's just a dream.

Owen No, it was a vision.

> *OWEN stops.*

Dolder You are trying to tell yourself something.

Owen And there are nuns.

Dolder What do they suggest to you.

Owen Penguins.

Dolder Penguins.

Owen But I save the children.

Dolder You save the children: save them from what.

Owen Death, dummy.

Dolder You don't think this means anything.

Owen Yes, now I know four things. I know that my voice doesn't change – but I still don't know why. I know that I'm God's instrument. I know when I'm going to die – and now a dream has shown me how I'm going to die, saving the children. I trust that God will help me, because what I'm supposed to do looks very hard.

JOHN picks up a diary and opens it, flicking through the pages.

Dolder Penguins.

John The dream, the dream…

Dolder Where do penguins live.

Owen The Unspeakable Outrage.

Merrill What is the Unspeakable Outrage.

Dolder Penguins live where it's cold.

Owen Him and His church, it's an insult to my mother.

Merrill What about your father.

Owen I know who my father is.

Dolder You don't believe that your father is really your father.

Merrill No, Owen, no.

Owen It's true.

Dolder How does this make you feel towards your mother.

John The dream, the dream.

Dolder (*Triumphantly.*) Like a penguin.

Owen He loves us all.

JOHN finds the page.

John The dream.

Reads from diary.

I never hear the explosion, what I always hear is the aftermath of an explosion –

Owen Always the aftermath –

John Ringing in my ears.

Owen And pieces of the sky falling, and bits of white – paper, plaster, floating down, shattered glass – no smoke, no flames, but the smell of burning, smouldering in the rubble, lying on the ground, children lost in the aftermath holding their ears, their ears are bleeding, they stand – children, crying, comforting, chattering, babbling, I can't understand, they're not American, reassuring, their voices the first human sounds since the explosion. They look at me – I know that I saved them but I don't know how, I know that something is wrong but I don't know what, I can't see me, I can't tell what's wrong but I can see it in their faces – the fear. Nuns, penguins, peer down, a sister of mercy kneels and takes me in her arms, I speak but I don't hear what I say, she understands, maybe she's American – and then I see all the blood, on her hands, on her face, spattered and splashing and it keeps on coming, she's soaking up the blood, my blood, covered in my blood and she smiles and raises her hand to make the sign of the cross over me and I reach out to stop her but I can't, I don't have any arms – she smiles and makes the sign of the cross and as she does I leave my body, leave all of this behind, just leave the world…and soon I'm looking down at them looking down at me – at what used to be me…and I'm above everything, above the palm trees, above the helicopters, above the sky, and the palm trees are so beautiful and it's so very hot, the air is hotter than any place I've ever been and I know I'm not in New Hampshire any more. Father, give me strength.

OWEN passes out.

Merrill (*To audience.*) Let us pray, let us pray for Owen Meany.

MERRILL prays. Exit DOLDER. OWEN descends.

Neatly folded US Army uniform and rifle placed centre stage.

Exit MERRILL.

JOHN turns to audience. As JOHN speaks, OWEN puts on uniform and picks up rifle.

John We tried to stop it…the Tet Offensive, Operation Rolling Thunder, Operation Tiger Hound, Operation Paul Revere – remember. Who remembers. Who cares. All those dead. And for what – the Dow Jones, the Footsie, the Hansing… But in 1967 there was still hope, we marched on the Pentagon demanding peace – remember – and again and again and again, Washington Boston New York – remember – before Watergate, before Ronald Reagan numbed the United States, before… Reagan said we were 'giving comfort and aid to the enemy', as president he didn't know who the enemy was and America still doesn't know – we wanted peace, we wanted it now, we were against the war and Owen joined the army.

Owen I have to go.

John But you're a pacifist.

Owen Of course I'm a pacifist, that's why I have to go.

John Go to Vietnam then and end up dead, like Harold Crosby.

Owen Who's Harold Crosby.

John He was the descending angel.

Owen Oh, him.

John You believe that God wants you to go to Vietnam.

Owen Yes.

John God told you.

Owen Yes, too fucking right, God told me – I had a dream – I keep on having this fucking dream, okay – okay – I don't want to go to Vietnam but I know that's where I have to be.

John It's just a dream.

Owen But you have no faith, that's your problem.

John It's only a dream.

Owen It's not your dream.

John Don't play around with me.

Owen I'm not playing around, you think I would have requested a combat assignment if I was playing around.

John You've requested combat assignment. Okay. Okay. You won't stop, I'm coming with you, I'll join up, I'll go to Vietnam with you.

Owen I won't let you die, Johnny.

John Did you say that, did you really say that.

Owen I won't let you die.

John I can't remember you saying that. Why.

Owen I save the children – I save lots of children, not soldiers, I wouldn't bother if they were soldiers – Vietnamese children, that's how I know where I am.

John You can't believe that.

Owen I do.

Enter TABITHA. Takes up position as statue.

John It's so childish, you can't believe that everything that pops into your head means something – that because you dream something it's going to happen, that you know what you're supposed to do.

Owen That isn't what faith is, I don't believe everything that pops into my head – faith is a little more selective than that.

John Like choosing to see what isn't there.

Owen Can you see the statue of Mary Magdalene.

John Stop playing around.

Owen Can you see her.

John No, it's too dark.

Owen But you know she's still there.

John Of course she's still there.

Owen You're sure.

John I'm sure.

Owen But you can't see her, how do you know she's actually still there if you can't actually see her.

John Because I know, okay – I just know.

Owen You have no doubt she's there.

John Of course I have no doubt.

Owen But you can't see her, you could be wrong.

John No, I'm not wrong – she's there, I know she's there.

Exit TABITHA.

Owen You absolutely know she's there, even though you can't see her.

John Yes.

Owen Well now you know how I feel about God, I can't see him, but I absolutely know he is there. Let's sink the shot.

John In the dark.

Owen We need to get it down to under three seconds.

John You go to Vietnam, I go too.

Owen Yes, you do Johnny – but not to fight.

John Nobody goes to Vietnam not to fight.

Owen You do.

John How do you know.

Owen Because you're in my dream. You're in the dream.

End of Act Two.

ACT THREE

Enter JOHN. Sleeps. Eva Cassidy's 'Wade in the Water', sung by TABITHA at a 1940s microphone in a flaming red dress. Enter US Army pall-bearers upstage carrying a coffin, followed by DAN and MERRILL. They place the coffin upstage centre. Exit pall-bearers. DAN and MERRILL stand in prayer at either end of the coffin. Dream. The sound of helicopters hovering and a large swirling fan flies in over centre stage. The ringing of a telephone cuts through the above. OWEN descends in Hawaiian shirt with a cocktail, smoking.

JOHN wakes.

John No.

Telephone stops ringing. Song stops. Stage clears of dream. Exit TABITHA. Microphone flown out. DAN, coffin and MERRILL remain upstage centre.

Owen Hello.

John Hello.

Owen I woke you up.

John No. Who is that.

Owen Owen.

John Owen.

Owen Can you meet me in Phoenix.

John Can I meet you in Phoenix.

Owen It's kind of an emergency.

John Who is this.

Owen There's been a body misplaced – California, they
thought it got lost in Vietnam but it just turned up in
Oakland – happens every holiday, someone goes to
sleep over the switch – you can always trust the US
Army to fuck it up with military precision – the body
belongs in Phoenix and I've got to deliver it for the
President with his condolences. Meet me in Phoenix.

John Owen.

Owen I've already booked us into a motel with air
conditioning, good TV, a great pool, we'll have a blast.

John Why.

Owen Why not – you don't have any plans, do you.

John Well, no.

Owen You can afford the 'plane fare, can't you.

John Well, yes.

Owen We can play tennis.

John I don't play tennis.

Owen We don't have to play tennis. You're my best friend.

John I'll be there.

*OWEN lies centre stage, sunglasses and a couple of beers.
JOHN opens diary. Reads.*

Owen There isn't time for me to go to Vietnam. I thought
I knew I was going there. I thought I knew the date too.

John (*Reads.*) But if I'm right about the date then I'm
wrong about it happening in Vietnam.

Owen And if I'm right about Vietnam then I'm wrong about the date. God is teaching me a lesson.

John (*Reads.*) Or maybe it really is just a dream.

Owen What's the book.

John Jude the Obscure.

OWEN offers him a beer. JOHN takes beer.

Owen Cheers.

John Cheers.

They drink.

Owen This is the life, pal.

John Yeah.

Owen Drinking beers sitting round the pool. I'm in the dying business, and this is one of the perks. Dying – it's a growth industry.

John It's the future.

Owen Everyone's future.

John To the future.

Owen Death.

They drink.

John What am I doing here.

Owen I don't know, all I know is that it's important you be here.

John Why Phoenix.

Owen I told you, I've got a body to deliver. Come on man lighten up, let your self off the hook, live a little.

John Yeah.

Owen Yeah, let's get laid.

John Yeah.

Owen You enjoy it.

John What, what do I enjoy.

Owen Nothing. Torturing yourself.

John No I don't.

Owen You believe in nothing and mistrust everything.

John You hate the Catholic Church.

Owen That's different.

John I believe in people.

Owen But you have no faith in them.

John What good has organised religion ever done anyone –

Owen (*Looking off.*) Look at that.

JOHN looks.

No, don't.

John You said.

Owen Not like that.

John They can't even agree on the same God.

Owen Maybe she's got a friend.

John All they create is misery.

Owen She's looking.

John Whose side is your God on in Vietnam.

Owen Anyone that needs Him.

John Don't be so fucking pious.

Owen I'm not. She is, she's looking.

John And God loves us all.

Owen Yes.

John He loves the torturer as well as his victim.

Owen Look at those legs.

John I hate your God.

Owen Just look, okay.

JOHN looks.

John At least Santa Claus leaves presents behind, God just gives us shit.

Owen She's coming over.

John No, she's not.

Owen Yes, she is.

OWEN stands ready to greet her.

John See, I told you.

Owen Where's she going.

John Canada.

Owen Promise me that's where you're going – promise me.

John I can't.

Owen You're so fucking selfish – you put yourself at the
centre of everything and end up feeling sorry for
yourself.

John You invent God and then claim to be rational.

Owen It's so fucking arrogant.

John And you're not.

Owen No.

John Oh, I give up.

Owen Yes, yes you have.

John No, I haven't.

Owen Yes you have.

John I haven't.

Owen You have.

John Arrrrrrrrrrgh!

Owen What, what's the matter.

John You – you always have to have the last word.

Owen No, I don't.

John Yes, you do.

Owen I don't.

John You do.

Pause.

Owen Not always. I'll get some more beer.

John I don't want any more beer.

Owen You don't know what you want.

John Yes I do.

Owen What, what do you want.

John I'll have another beer.

Exit OWEN.

Dan Amen.

John Why did you do that, what am I doing here, why do you always make me feel like this.

DAN turns away from coffin.

Dan John, he's been dead for twenty years.

John God gives life, God takes life, but what else does He do.

Dan Forgive it. Forgive and forget – and come home.

Merrill (*Over coffin.*) Earth to earth, ashes to ashes, dust to dust.

John Canada is my home – all Americans should be forced to live in another country, then maybe they'll understand why the rest of the world hates us.

Dan Let bygones be bygones – not even Owen would still be angry after twenty years in exile. Do you think Owen Meany would have blamed the whole country for what happened to him. That was madness: this is madness too. Come home.

JOHN opens diary.

Merrill I am the ressurrection and the life, saith the Lord –

John (*Reads.*) Nam soon – lie down…

Merrill He that believeth in me, though he were dead, yet shall he live.

John (*Reads.*) Doong sa – don't be afraid…

Merrill And whosoever liveth and believeth in me shall never die.

John (*Reads.*) Top right hand drawer…

Merrill Amen.

John He knew, he knew everything – nam soon, doong sa – it's written here, here in his diary – that's why his voice never changed – so that they understood him, so they could hear – I heard it, I saw it happen – you've got to believe it, believe me.

Dan I believe you.

John But do you believe that it was a miracle.

Dan Do you.

Silence.

John Yes, yes – I have to, I've got no choice, he gave me no choice –

MERRILL turns away from coffin and to JOHN.

Merrill To believe it – I mean all of it, to b-b-b-believe everything…well that takes more faith than I've got.

John If I can believe it, why can't you.

Merrill You haven't l-l-l-lived with belief and with unbelief, you haven't been f-f-f-full of faith and then filled with d-d-d-doubt.

John (*To self.*) Everyday, everyday I doubt, the ground beneath my feet and I fall and nothing is certain…and I'm falling – (*To MERRILL.*) But he knew, he knew everything – nam soon, doong sa – it was a miracle.

Merrill So you're going to Canada.

John Yes.

Merrill Because of Owen.

John I promised him.

Dan Come home, John.

Merrill Go to Canada then.

Dan It's been twenty years.

Merrill You think you witnessed a miracle.

John It was a miracle.

Merrill And now you believe.

John No – yes, I have to.

Dan Because you need to.

John No.

Merrill Real miracles don't c-c-c-cause faith out of thin air, you have to have faith already to believe in real miracles.

John No.

Dan Come home, John.

John He had a vision.

Merrill And you ascribe that to the hand of God.

John I know what I saw.

Merrill But you don't believe in God – look at you.

John You don't believe in God.

Dan I don't feel strongly either way.

John But you go to church every Sunday.

Dan Because it reminds me of your mother.

Exit DAN and MERRILL.

Silence.

John It was a miracle.

Offstage explosion of TNT. The MEANYS as in Act One, listening to phonograph. MR MEANY sat with green army duffle bag at his feet. Offstage explosion of TNT. MR MEANY turns off phonograph.

Mr Meany Come in, son, we've been expecting you.

JOHN steps into the MEANYS' front room.

Damn phonograph.

MR MEANY sits.

Mrs Meany Your mother was an angel.

Silence.

Mr Meany They gave us fifty thousand dollars, cash. Where's the government get that kind of money from.

John I don't know.

Mr Meany Not for every dead soldier.

John They think very highly of him.

Mr Meany Somebody does. How is your grandmother.

John Fine, sir, just fine.

Mr Meany Give her my regards. Normally I don't take charity but in this case I'm making an exception.

Mrs Meany Fifty thousand dollars.

Mr Meany It's a lot of money.

Mrs Meany Not much for a life.

Mr Meany Don't mind her, son, she's a pessimist.

Mrs Meany It's not me that's going to hell.

Mr Meany You know what a pessimist is, son.

John Yes, sir.

Mr Meany I'll tell you what a pessimist is – that is a pessimist.

Mrs Meany At least I say my prayers.

Mr Meany A lot of good Owen's praying done him.

Silence.

John Would you like me to unpack his bag.

Mr Meany I'd be happy if you would.

OWEN appears upstage in dim golden light as if under a halo. JOHN takes duffle bag. Opens it. Takes out a baseball bat, a Bible and a book.

It ain't there. Look all you want but you won't find it. Look in his room too, it ain't there neither…it never was – I know, I've been looking for it for years. Whoever clung on to that baseball it wasn't Owen.

John I just assumed…

Mr Meany Me too. What's the book.

John St Thomas Aquinas.

Owen Since everything that is moved functions as a sort
of instrument of the first mover, if there was no first
mover, then whatever things are in motion would be
simply instruments…it is ridiculous to suppose that
instruments are moved but not by any principal agent.
This would be like supposing that the construction of a
wooden box could be accomplished by putting a saw or
a hatchet to work without any carpenter to use them.
Therefore, there must be a first mover existing above all
– and this we call God. Top right hand drawer,
remember.

Light fades on OWEN.

John What.

Mr Meany What's the book.

John (*Reads spine of book.*) *A Demonstration of God's Existence
from Motion.*

Mr Meany He wasn't natural.

John He was very special.

Mr Meany No, I mean he wasn't natural, he wasn't normal,
he was born…different.

Mrs Meany No, stop…they said not to.

Mr Meany What do I care about Him and His Church – I
mean he was born unnaturally, like the Christ child
…me and his mother –

Mrs Meany Don't.

Mr Meany We didn't ever do it –

Mrs Meany Stop.

Mr Meany She just conceived a child. I am not Owen's father. That was the first outrage.

Mrs Meany God will strike you dead.

Mr Meany I already am.

Mrs Meany He doesn't believe you, no one ever does.

John You're saying that Owen was a virgin birth.

Mr Meany She was a virgin – yes.

Mrs Meany They never, never, never, never believe you.

Mr Meany Be quiet, woman.

John There couldn't have been an accident…

Mr Meany I told you, we never did it – the only person my wife ever did it with is God.

Mrs Meany Stop it.

John You believe –

Mr Meany It's true.

Mrs Meany I did nothing.

John You really believe…

Mr Meany Don't you be like those damn priests. They believe *that* story but they wouldn't listen to *this* one. They even teach that other story but they tell us our story is worse than some kinda sin.

Mrs Meany Owen was no sin.

John No, he wasn't.

Mr Meany I went from one church to the next – those Catholics…all I knew was granite, we lived in Concord – there wasn't no Catholic in Concord we could talk to. It was an outrage the things they said to us –

Mrs Meany I did nothing wrong.

Mr Meany So we moved to Barre.

Mrs Meany I loved my son, I prayed to God.

Mr Meany Be quiet. But the Catholic Church in Barre was no different, they made out like we was blaspheming the Bible, like we was trying to make up our own religion or something. So we left Barre and settled in Gravesend where the granite ain't so good and said nothing – that's when me, God and the Church parted company. It was an outrage.

Mrs Meany Unspeakable outrage.

Mr Meany When Owen was old enough –

Mrs Meany Stop, enough.

Mr Meany I said, be quiet.

John You told Owen.

Mr Meany When we thought he was old enough.

John And when was that.

Mr Meany I guess he was ten or eleven – about the time he hit that ball. I got something I want to show you.

MR MEANY and JOHN walk over to a large object under a dust-sheet.

Mrs Meany (*Shouts after them.*) Stop.

Mr Meany Pay no attention, she's plain ignorant. Don't you just hate ignorance, son.

John Yes, yes I do.

Exit MRS MEANY.

The MEANYS' house is cleared.

Mr Meany When she's dead I'm getting a dog.

MR MEANY rips off dust cover, revealing a granite gravestone. Written in large letters, 'First Lt. Paul O Meany, Jr. 12/24/42 to 03/31/68 In aeternum.' MR MEANY reads it out loud.

John Very fine, mighty fine work, sir – with the diamond wheel.

Mr Meany That ain't my work, that's Owen's work.

John So you just added the date, the date of his death.

Mr Meany I added nothing. He did it when he was last on leave.

Exit MR MEANY. Strike gravestone. Enter OWEN in military uniform with black armband. Carrying a small triangular box.

Owen Ready.

John No, no, I'm not ready, not yet.

OWEN gives JOHN a black armband. JOHN puts it on.

Owen Now you look acceptably official.

OWEN gives box to JOHN.

And you get to carry the box.

John What's in it.

Owen The Stars and Stripes.

Enter MAJOR RAWLS. He and OWEN salute and stand at ease.

Enter the JARVIT family. FATHER, MOTHER, pregnant DAUGHTER and youngest SON in jungle fatigues, a machete hanging from his army belt and a sheathed bayonet, wearing basketball shoes. They stand in a line waiting. Enter a forklift truck driven by a US soldier. The truck picks up the coffin from upstage centre. Raises coffin. Drives downstage centre. Lowers coffin in front of family.

Mother Fuck.

DAUGHTER cries. The BOY spits tobacco juice.

Daughter Stop doing that.

Boy Fuck you.

Father Don't you speak to your sister like that.

Boy Fuck you – she's not my sister, she's my half-sister

Mother Don't speak to your father like that.

Boy He's not my father – you asshole.

Father Don't you call your mother an asshole.

BOY takes out machete and unsheathes bayonet.

Boy You're both assholes.

DAUGHTER cries. BOY spits tobacco juice in FATHER's direction. Silence.

Owen (*Shrill piercing voice.*) I like that sheath – for the bayonet, you made it yourself.

DAUGHTER stops crying.

Boy Who the fuck are you, motherfucker.

Rawls This is the casualty officer. This is Lieutenant Meany.

Boy I want to hear the dwarf say it.

Owen I'm Lieutenant Meany, what's your name.

OWEN offers his hand to shake.

Boy What's wrong with your voice.

Owen Nothing. What's the matter with you. You want to dress up and play soldier – don't you know how to speak to an officer.

Boy Yes sir.

Owen Put those weapons away. Is that your brother I just brought home.

Boy Yes sir.

Owen I'm sorry that your brother is dead.

Boy Yeah, me too sir.

Owen Then pay him some attention.

Boy Yes sir.

BOY puts away bayonet and machete.

Owen (*To DAUGHTER.*) I'm sorry about your brother.

Daughter My half-brother.

Boy He was my brother.

Owen What's your name.

Boy Fuck you.

Owen You're talking to an officer.

Boy Fuck you, sir.

Owen That's better.

Rawls Keep the bayonet in its sheath.

Boy Shit, this is nothing – I got a whole fucking armoury at home, and two chinkie shit commie grenades all courtesy of good ol' Frank.

Owen Who's Frank.

Boy The dummy in the box, shit-head, sir.

Owen I'm sorry.

Mother It was his third tour of duty.

Owen I'm sorry.

Boy When I'm seventeen I'm going to join the army and get me a necklace of real live gook ears. How come you ain't in 'Nam, sir – you too small or something else.

Rawls Lieutenant Meany has requested a transfer to Vietnam, he's scheduled to go there.

Boy (*To RAWLS.*) How come you ain't over there.

Owen How come you ain't over there, sir.

Boy How come you ain't over there, sir.

Rawls I've already been. I said sheath that bayonet, boy.

Boy How come you ain't back there.

Rawls I've got a better job here.

Mother Somebody got to stay home and do the dirty jobs son, that's just the way it is.

Boy Sure is, ma.

Owen When you get in the army, what kind of job do you think you'll have –

Boy Killing little chinkie-shit people with funny voices.

Owen With an attitude like that you're not going to war, you're going to jail – you don't have to be smart to go to Vietnam, but you have to be smarter than you.

Boy I don't need the fucking army, sir – I got enough weapons to start a war of my own.

Rawls Keep that bayonet in its sheath son, or I'll have no choice but to break your fucking neck.

Boy Who's the dummy without a uniform.

Owen He's Intelligence.

Boy You carry a gun.

Owen Not that kind of intelligence.

Boy Oh.

BOY spits. DAUGHTER cries.

Owen Who do I give the flag to.

Father It ain't got nothing to do with me.

OWEN presents box to MOTHER.

Owen It is my privilege, mam, to present to you our country's flag in grateful appreciation for the service rendered to this nation by your son.

MOTHER doesn't take flag and spits in OWEN's face. OWEN salutes.

Boy Keep your dumb fucking flag, asshole.

Mother And keep away from my son's funeral, I don't want it soiled by the military.

Coffin raised up by fork-lift truck. Exit fork-lift truck with coffin. Exit JARVIT FAMILY.

Rawls Trailer trash inbreeds – they should just ship the whole damn family out to Vietnam and to hell with them, save us all the trouble – they're beyond saving.

Owen It's not up to you or me, sir – it's not up to us, who's beyond saving.

Rawls You're too good for this world, Meany.

Owen Yes, sir, Major Rawls, sir.

Exit RAWLS. OWEN handed microphone and stand.

(*As Lenny Bruce.*) Could someone tell me what's the matter with this fucking country, there is such a stupid get even mentality – hey, fuck you man – hey, and you – there is such a sadistic anger. Is this country so huge that it needs to oversimplify everything. I mean, look at the war: either we have a strategy to 'win' it, which makes us – in the world's view – murderers; or else we are dying, without fighting to win. Look at what we call

'Foreign Policy': our 'Foreign Policy' is a euphemism for public relations and our public relations get worse and worse, we're being defeated and we're not good losers. Hey, sit the fuck down, I'm not finished – and look at what we call 'religion' – you know what I'm saying – turn on any television on any Sunday morning, see the choirs of the poor and uneducated – ahh – and then look at the dumb-shit mother-fucking asshole preacher they're listening to. He's got VD, man. No, VFD – Verbal Fucking Diarrhea – and you better duck 'cos it's coming your way, 'cos soon he's gonna be in the White House, soon he's gonna be on the Supreme Fucking Court, and then – we'll all be covered in shit. And one day, one day there will come an epidemic – I'll bet on some real humdinger of a sexual disease – and what will our peerless leaders, our heads of church and state, what will they say to us, how will they tell us – you can be sure they won't cure us – but how will they comfort us. Just turn on the TV – and here's what our peerless leaders, our heads of church and state will say: they'll say, ' I told you so!' they'll say, 'That's what you get for fucking around – I told you not to do it until you got married.' Doesn't anyone listen (*Bangs microphone.*) – hello – hello – doesn't anyone see what these simpletons are up to. These self-righteous, self-serving, self-promoting, self-satisfying, self-fucking-hating fanatics – they're not 'religious' – the only cross they know is the one they use to sign the company cheque with – their agenda is not 'morality' – the only principle they remember is the one who used to beat em. But that's where this country is headed – it's headed toward oversimplification. Over-simpli-fication. You want to see the president of the future. You wanna see him. Turn on any television on any Sunday morning – find one of those holy rollers – that's him, that's the new Mister President! And do you want to see the future of all those kids who are going to fall through the cracks of this great, big, sloppy society of ours. Well I just met him – he's a tall, skinny fifteen-year-old boy with a machete. He's pretty scary. What's wrong with him is what's wrong with the TV evangelist – our future president. What's wrong with both of them is that they're so sure they're right! That's pretty scary – the future, I think, looks pretty fucking scary.

John So, what do you want to do.

Owen It doesn't matter, let's just have a good time.

OWEN hands mic stand off stage. Enter MERRILL. Sits in swivel chair.

John He finished his own gravestone more than half a year before he died.

Merrill (*From swivel chair.*) If you can believe Mr Meany, the man is a monster of superstition – and as for the mother, well – she may simply be r-r-r-retarded. That they would believe Owen was a virgin birth is monstrous. But that they would tell him –

John Owen talked to you about it.

Merrill All the time.

John And what did you tell him.

Merrill Certainly not that I thought that he was the second Christ.

John But what did he say.

OWEN stands between them.

Owen I don't believe I am Jesus, but if you can believe in one virgin birth, why not in another.

John That sounds like Owen.

Owen I believe that there is a purpose to everything that happens to me, that God has meant for the story of my life to have some meaning.

Merrill He believed that God had p-p-p-picked him.

John Do you believe that.

Merrill You want to call Owen and everything that happened to him a m-m-m-miracle.

Owen Well it is.

Merrill Don't confuse your grief with genuine religious belief.

Owen What do you believe.

Merrill About Owen.

John No, not just Owen –

Owen It doesn't seem to me that you believe very much in God, it seems to me that your doubt has taken control of you.

Merrill Yes that's true – that's what Owen thought about m-m-m-me.

Owen Look in the desk.

John What are you going to say about him at his funeral.

Owen Top right hand drawer, remember.

Merrill Top right hand drawer, remember.

MERRILL holds out his right hand. OWEN places a baseball in it. MERRILL gives JOHN the baseball.

Forgive me, my s-s-s-son.

Silence.

Forgive me.

Silence.

Owen Forgive him.

John No.

Silence.

No. It was you she was waving at.

Merrill Yes.

John My father.

Merrill There are three things in this life of which I am certain – I was born, I will die, you are my son.

John No.

Merrill Yes.

John No.

Merrill She waved...strolling carelessly along the third baseline and she didn't seem to care and I prayed to God that your mother would drop dead, and it was at that moment Owen hit the next pitch and she dropped dead – I'm guilty, I'm responsible, it's the only time God has ever listened to me – I killed your mother. F-f-f-forgive me.

John No.

Exit MERRILL.

Owen You'll regret that.

JOHN throws baseball offstage.

John I need to sleep, I don't sleep, let me sleep, please God let me sleep…

Drops to knees and prays.

Blessed are the poor in spirit… Blessed are the meek. Blessed are the pure in heart, for they shall see God… but will it help them – what good will it do, what good did it do you… Wasn't my mother enough.

Pinball machine. Enter MAJOR RAWLS with small case. RAWLS gives case to OWEN. RAWLS goes to pinball machine and plays pinball throughout.

Owen Ready.

John No.

Owen You want asprin.

John No.

Owen I'll get you asprin.

John I don't want asprin.

Owen You shouldn't drink tequila.

John I like tequila.

Owen You drank a whole bottle, on your own.

John I like tequila.

Owen Tequila doesn't like you.

John It was something I ate, alright.

Owen Alright. You'll miss your plane. I hate fucking airports.

John I enjoyed Phoenix.

Owen Nothing happened.

John We got drunk.

Owen Yeah.

John Yeah.

They laugh.

What's the matter.

Owen Nothing. Maybe it will happen on the plane.

John What.

Owen Nothing.

John You okay.

Owen I'm okay. I had a dream that's all. Maybe it was just a crazy dream. Who the fuck knows what God knows. Maybe I should see a psychiatrist.

John You're still drunk.

Owen Yeah. We never practiced the shot.

John I never want to have to practice that shot again.

Owen After today you won't have to.

OWEN checks around.

You'll miss your plane.

John Yeah.

Owen See you later, pal.

John Yeah, see you later.

They embrace.

Enter NUNS.

What, what is it. They're just penguins.

Owen Here they come.

John Nuns.

Owen It's them.

Nun One Officer.

Owen Yes, mam, how may I help you.

Nun One Some of the children in our care need to use the men's room, we wondered if you'd be so kind.

Owen Children, yes of course, the children.

Nun One Yes.

Owen By the palm trees.

Nun One Yes, by the palm trees.

Owen In the shade under a hot sun, and the helicopters.

Nun One Would you be so kind, lieutenant.

Owen Certainly, mam, only too happy, mam.

Nun One We'll wait outside.

Exit NUNS.

Owen Come with me.

John I'll miss my plane.

Owen Leave the bag.

JOHN picks up case. OWEN goes as if to exit. Turns back and walks round to meet JOHN from the other side. JOHN turns to face OWEN. As OWEN walks round and JOHN turns, the NUNS walk upstage, turn their backs to audience and kneel as in prayer. As they kneel, they disrobe so that they look like Vietnamese children from the back. JOHN puts case down.

I said to leave the bag.

John What's wrong.

Owen Stand here. Stand here. Now look, look up – see the window, you see the window ledge.

John No.

Owen See the window ledge.

John I see it.

Owen Ten foot up, that's where we're aiming for.

John Owen.

Enter JARVIT BOY with grenade.

Owen Hello, Dick.

Boy That ain't my name, you little motherfucker.

Owen (*To children.*) Doong sa.

Child Don't be afraid

Owen Doong sa, doong sa.

Boy This is just the place for you to die with all these fucking little gooks – with their fucking little dinks.

Owen (*Shrill.*) Nam soon.

Child Lie down.

Vietnamese children fall to floor.

Owen Nam soon, nam soon.

Child Lie down, lie down.

Owen Now I know why my voice never changes, do you see why.

John Yes.

Owen We have just four seconds. You'll never get to Vietnam, Dick.

BOY rips the fuse cord from the grenade and tosses it to JOHN. JOHN catches grenade.

Boy Think fast, Mr Fucking Intelligence Man.

JARVIT BOY runs off past RAWLS at pinball machine. RAWLS catches BOY.

Rawls What have you done, you fuckface.

RAWLS takes machete off BOY and breaks the BOY's neck.

Owen Ready.

John Ready.

JOHN stands below where OWEN indicated the window is. JOHN throws grenade to OWEN. OWEN catches grenade.

OWEN runs towards JOHN, leaps into his arms and JOHN pushes him high up into the air. OWEN flies up towards the ledge, higher than we have ever seen him fly before.

We had about two seconds left to live, but he soared far above my arms, straight up, never turning and instead of neatly dropping the grenade and leaving it on the window ledge, he got hold of the ledge with both hands, pinning the grenade against the ledge and trapping it there safely with his hands and forearms. He clung there for less than a second. Then the grenade detonated. And he saved the children. And it was done.

Exit CHILDREN. OWEN and JOHN alone.

I never hear the explosion, what I hear is the aftermath of an explosion, always the aftermath ringing in my ears and pieces of the sky falling, and bits of white – paper, plaster, floating down, shattered glass – no smoke, no flames, but the smell of burning, smouldering in the rubble, lying on the ground, children lost in the aftermath holding their ears, their ears are bleeding, they stand – children, crying, comforting, chattering, babbling, their voices the first human sounds since the explosion. They look at me, as I had looked at Owen; a boy with a wrecked voice, the smallest person I ever knew, the instrument of my mother's death, the reason I believe in God, a sister of mercy covered in blood, soaking up the blood, his blood, blood on her face, blood on her hands – I stand over them, alone, in the heat, in the dust, and he looked up –

Pause.

Faith and prayer, John, faith and prayer.

Exit OWEN.

And he was gone.

Silence.

There's a prayer I say most often for Owen. It's one of the little prayers he said for my mother, 'Into paradise may the angels lead you, Father of all we pray to you for those we love but see no longer,' I'm always saying prayers for Owen Meany. O God – please give him back. I shall keep on asking you.

The End.